IGOR PRESNYAKOV'S
SOLO GUITAR
SONGBOOK

Music transcriptions by Pete Billmann and Jeff Jacobson

Cover photo: Svjatoslav Presnyakov

ISBN 978-1-5400-2152-6

Visit Hal Leonard Online at
www.halleonard.com

Contact us:
Hal Leonard
7777 West Bluemound Road
Milwaukee, WI 53213
Email: info@halleonard.com

In Europe, contact:
Hal Leonard Europe Limited
42 Wigmore Street
Marylebone, London, W1U 2RN
Email: info@halleonardeurope.com

In Australia, contact:
Hal Leonard Australia Pty. Ltd.
4 Lentara Court
Cheltenham, Victoria, 3192 Australia
Email: info@halleonard.com.au

Aerials

Words and Music by Daron Malakian and Serj Tankian

Drop D tuning, down 1 step:
(low to high) C-G-C-F-A-D

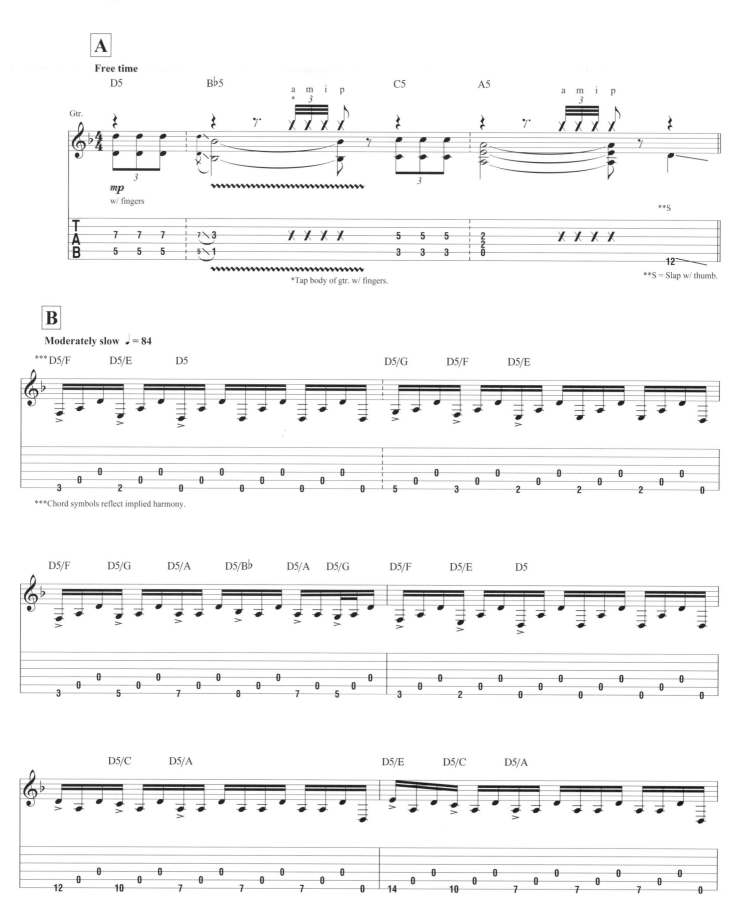

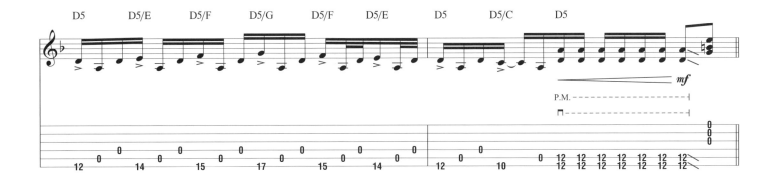

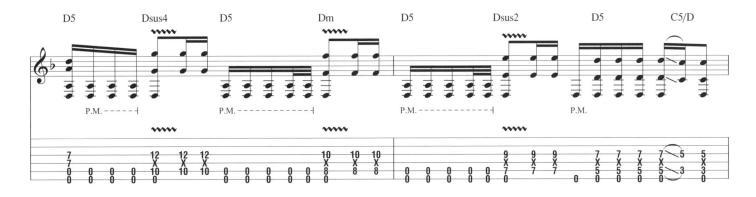

*Strum as if holding a pick, next 8 meas.

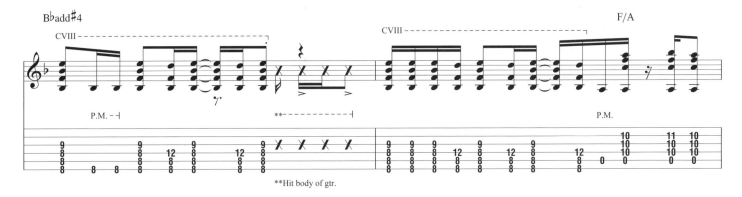

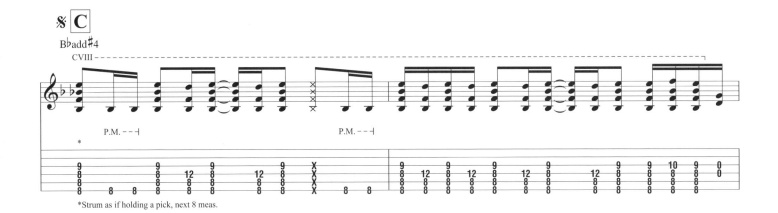

**Hit body of gtr.

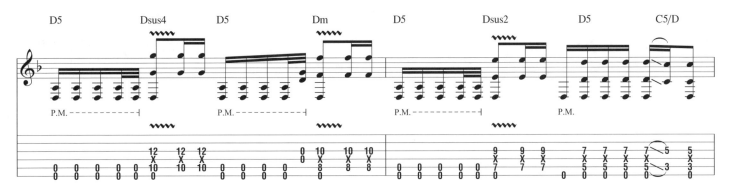

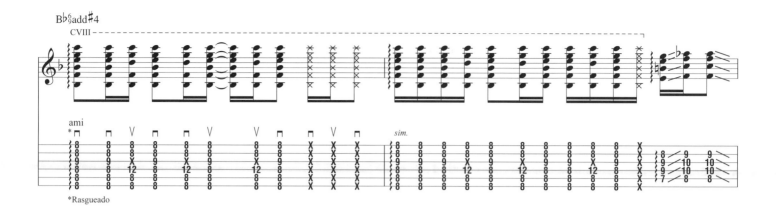

*Rasgueado

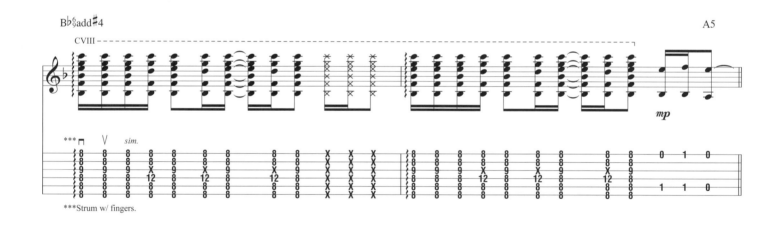

**Strum as if holding a pick, next 2 meas.

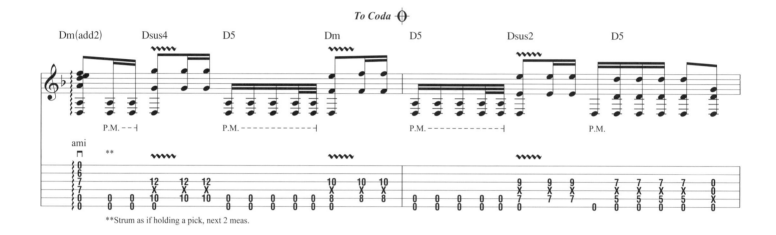

***Strum w/ fingers.

D

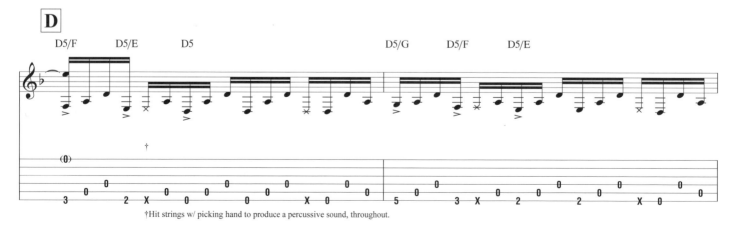

†Hit strings w/ picking hand to produce a percussive sound, throughout.

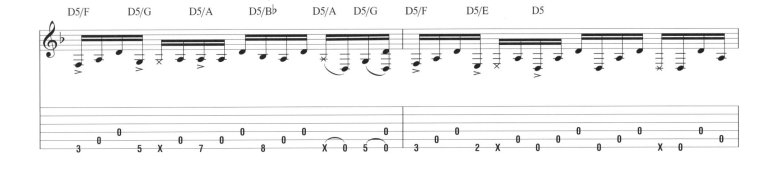

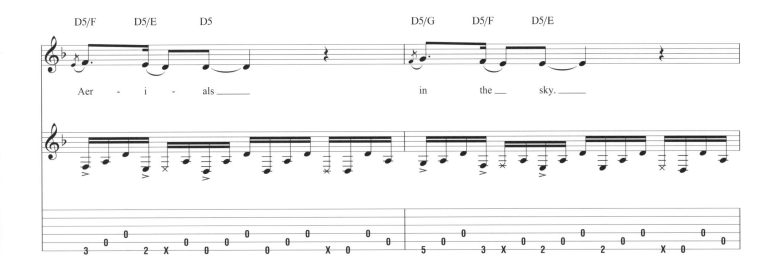

Aer - i - als _____ in the ___ sky. _____

D.S. al Coda

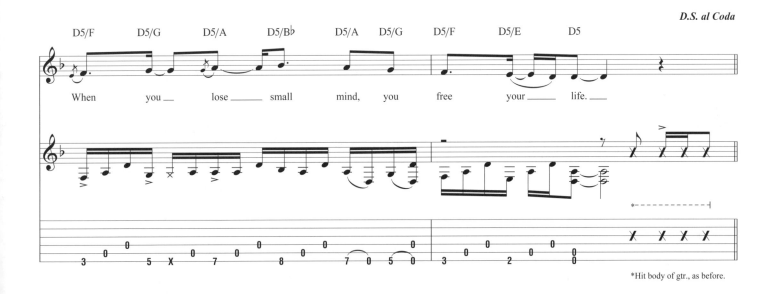

When you ___ lose _____ small mind, you free your ___ life.

*Hit body of gtr., as before.

Coda

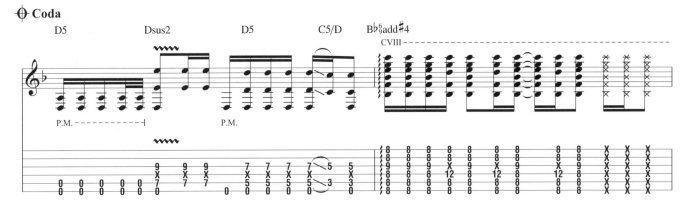

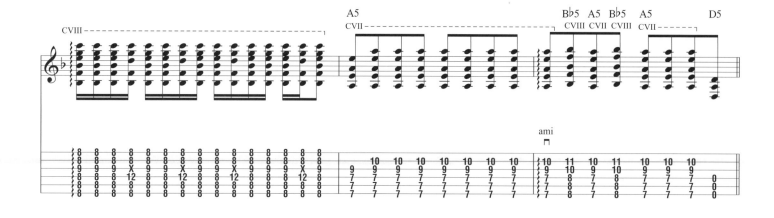

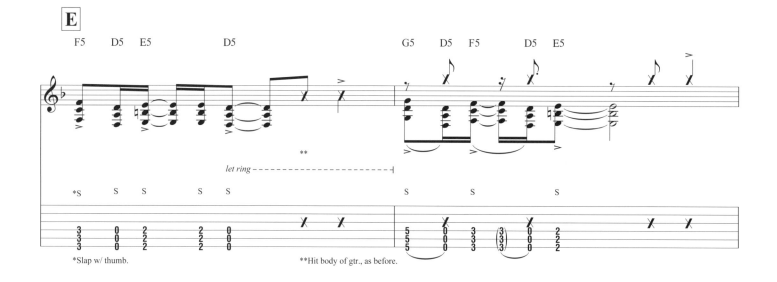

*Slap w/ thumb.   **Hit body of gtr., as before.

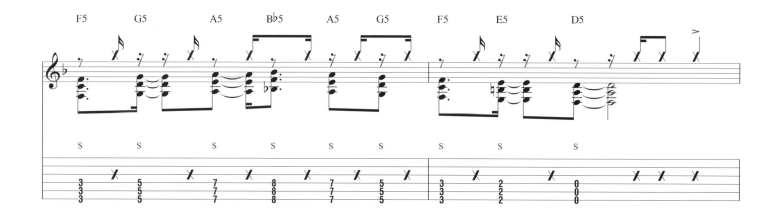

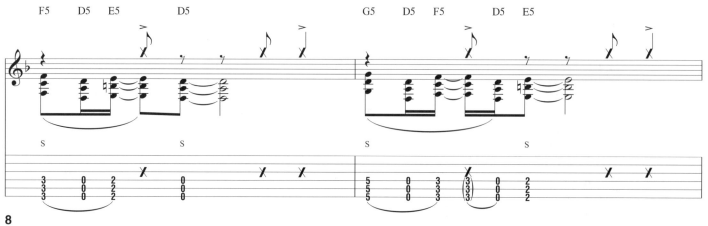

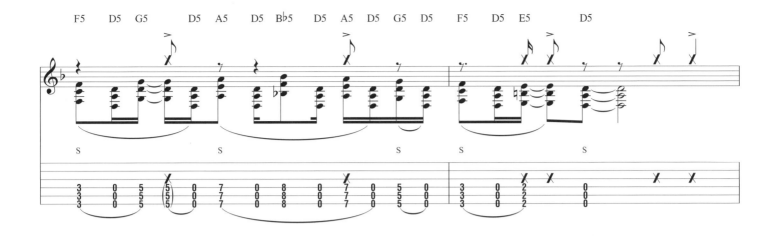

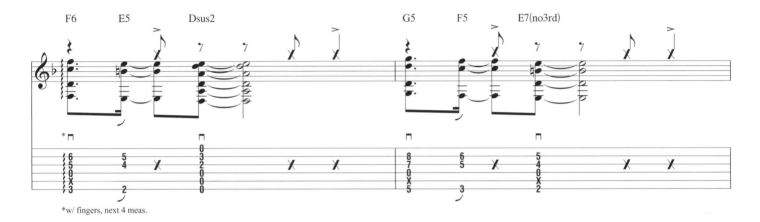

*w/ fingers, next 4 meas.

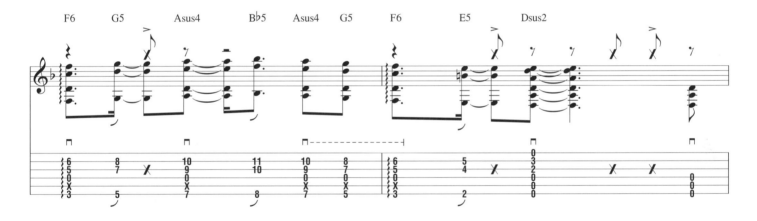

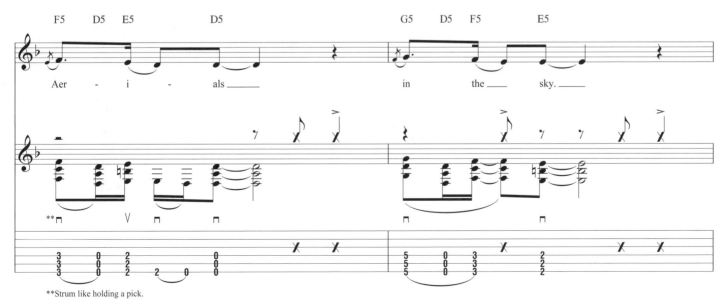

Aer - i - als _____ in the _____ sky. _____

**Strum like holding a pick.

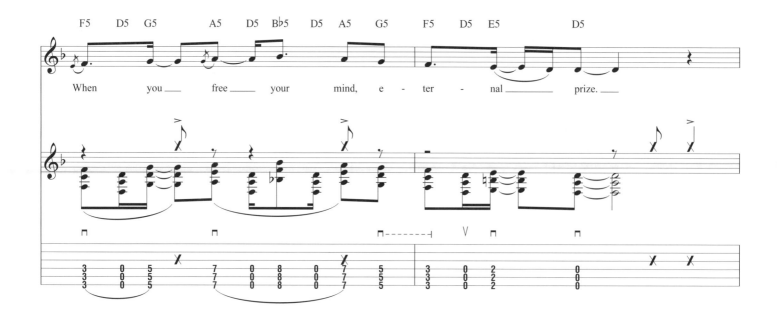

When you ___ free ___ your mind, e - ter - nal ___ prize. ___

*Strum w/ fingers.

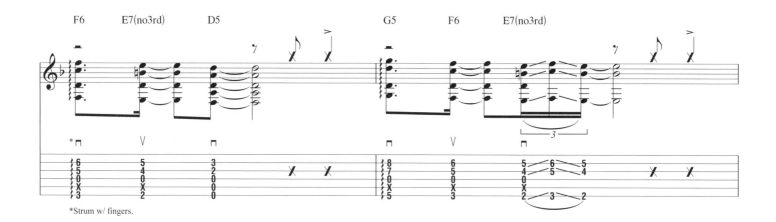

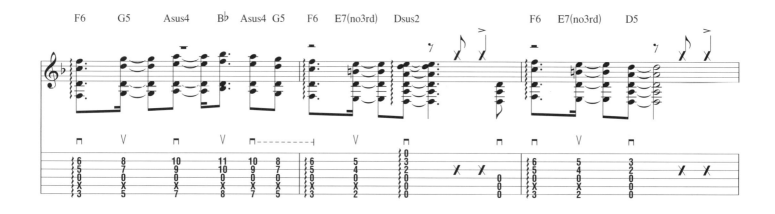

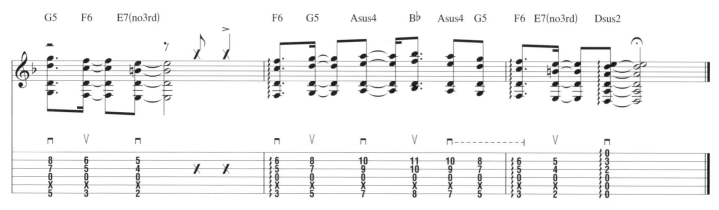

Ain't No Sunshine

Words and Music by Bill Withers

Tune down 1 step:
(low to high) D-G-C-F-A-D

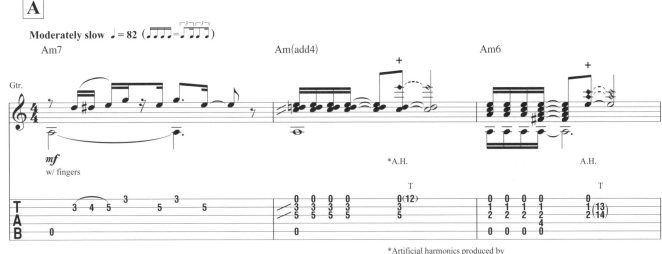

*Artificial harmonics produced by
tapping strings 12 frets above fretted notes.

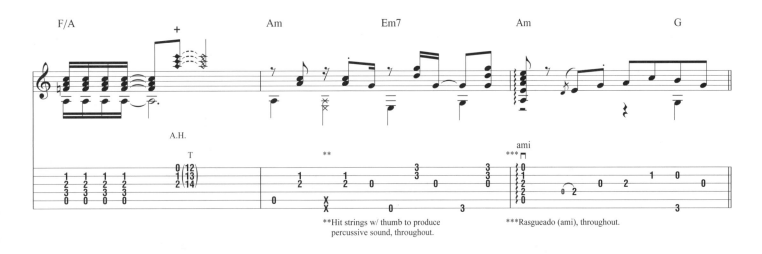

**Hit strings w/ thumb to produce
percussive sound, throughout.

***Rasgueado (ami), throughout.

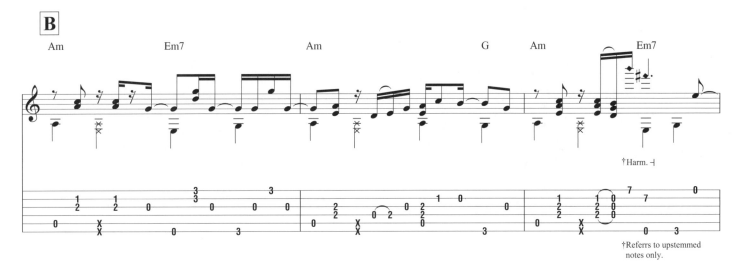

†Referrs to upstemmed
notes only.

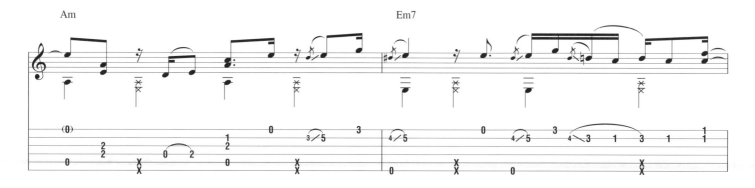

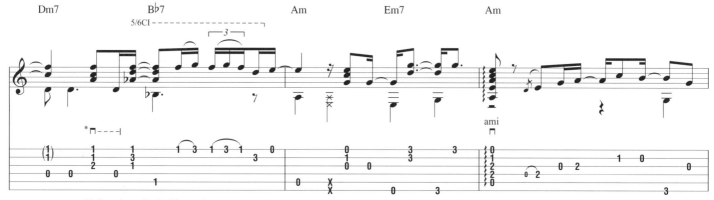

*Strike strings w/ back of fingernail.

**Harm.

**Refers to upstemmed notes only.

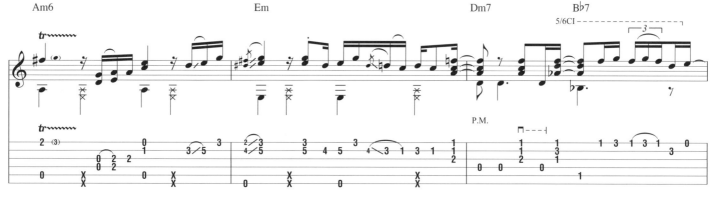

P.M.

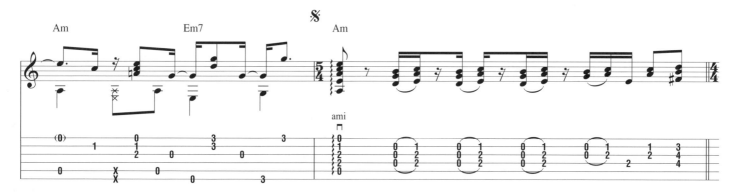

C

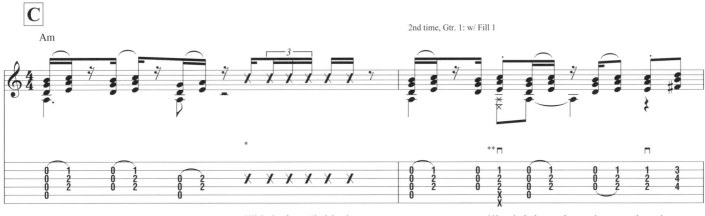

2nd time, Gtr. 1: w/ Fill 1

*Hit body of gtr. w/ both hands
to create percussive sounds, throughout.

**In a single downstroke, sound upstemmed notes by
striking strings w/ backs of fingernails while slapping
thumb against strings to produce a percussive sound
(downstemmed notes), throughout.

***w/ fingers

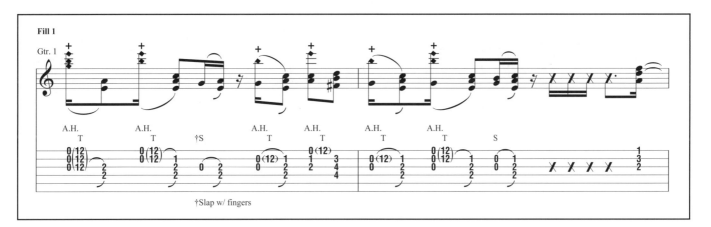

†Slap w/ fingers

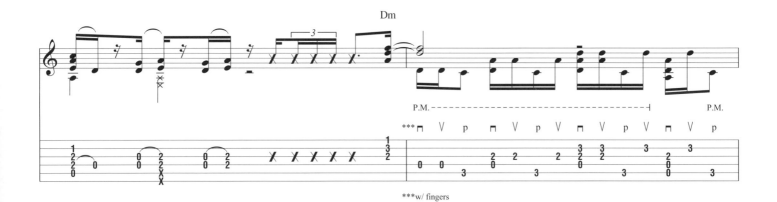

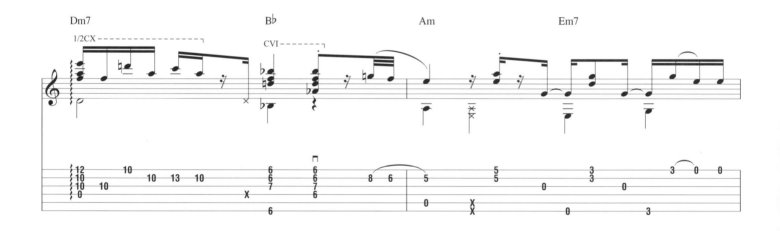

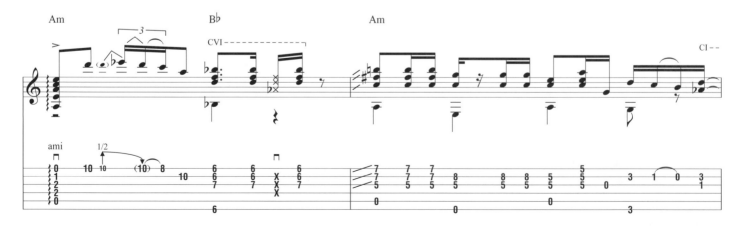

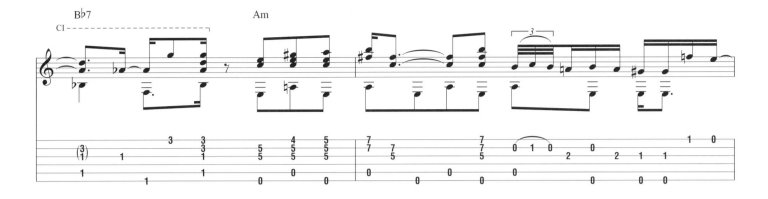

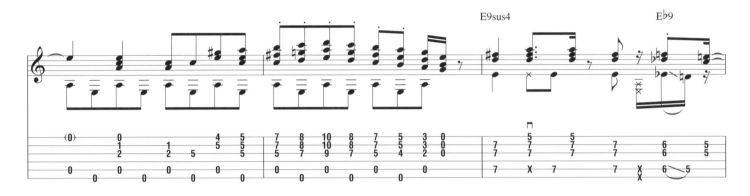

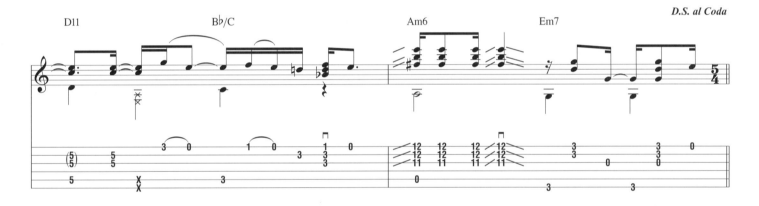

Careless Whisper

Words and Music by George Michael and Andrew Ridgeley

Tune down 1 step:
(low to high) D-G-C-F-A-D

*Hit body of gtr. w/ right hand
to create percussive sound.

**Hit strings w/ thumb to produce percussive
sound throughout, except where indicated.

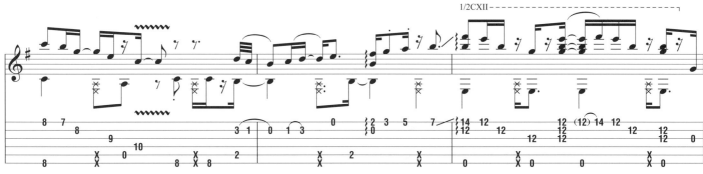

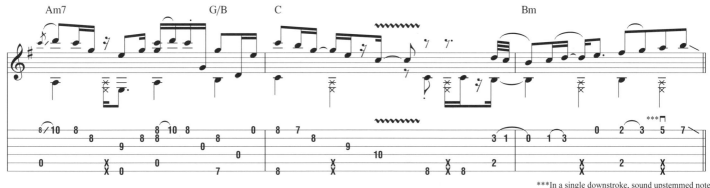

***In a single downstroke, sound upstemmed note
by striking string w/ back of fingernail while
slapping thumb against strings to produce a
percussive sound (downstemmed notes).

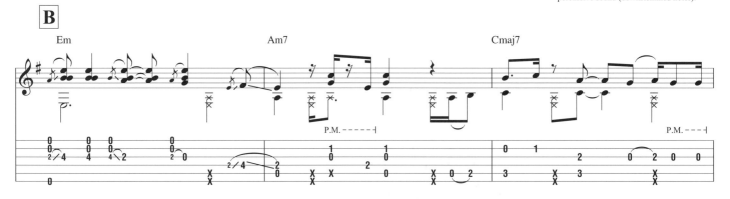

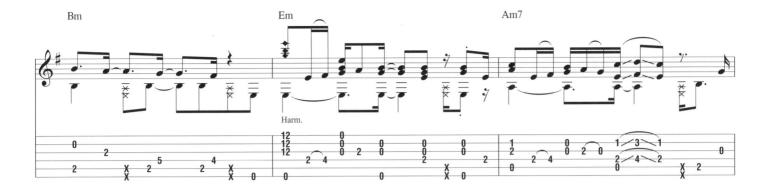

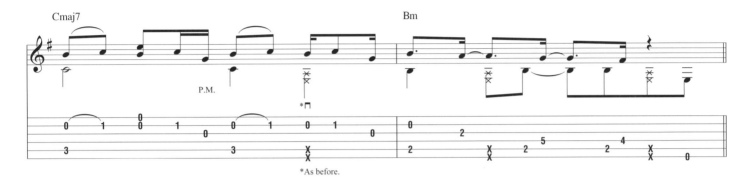

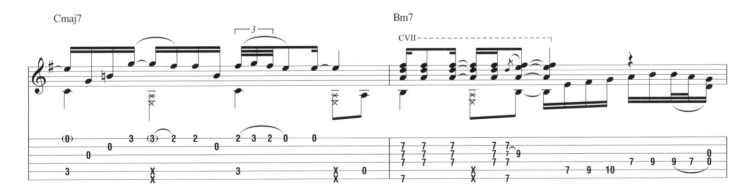

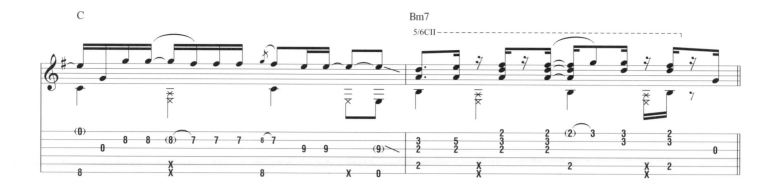

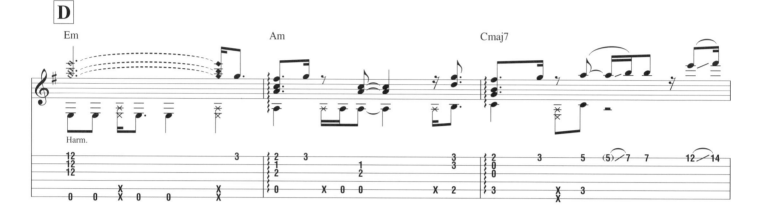

*Strum as if holding a pick.

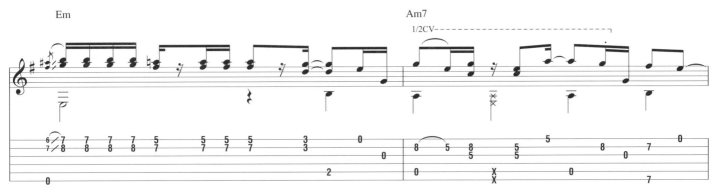

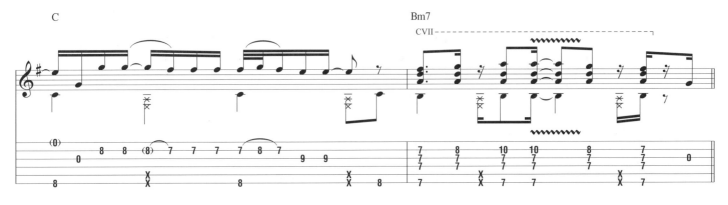

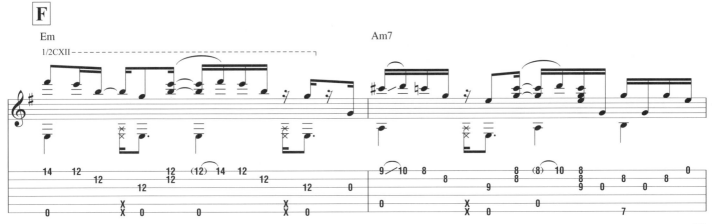

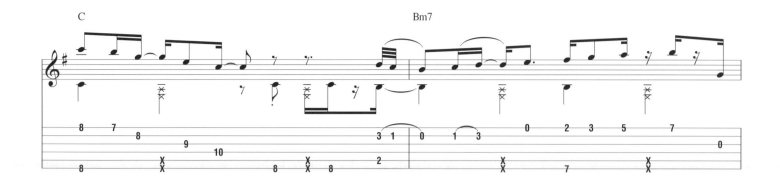

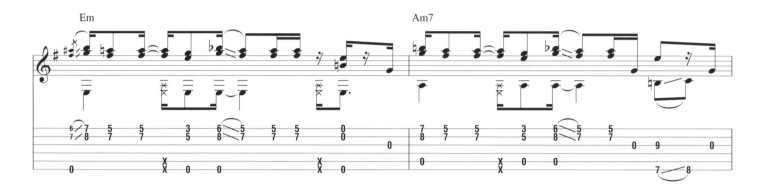

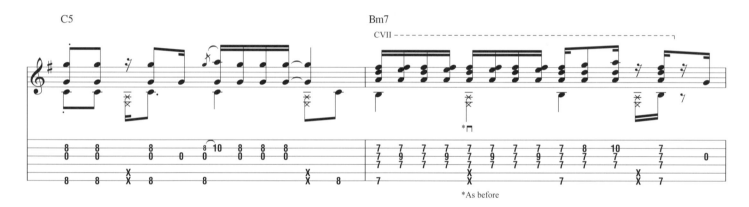

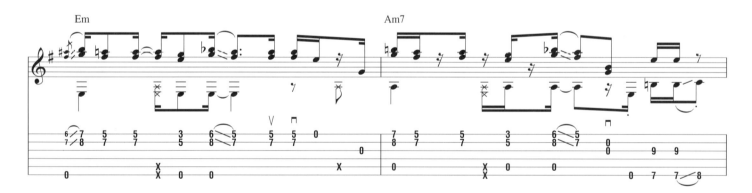

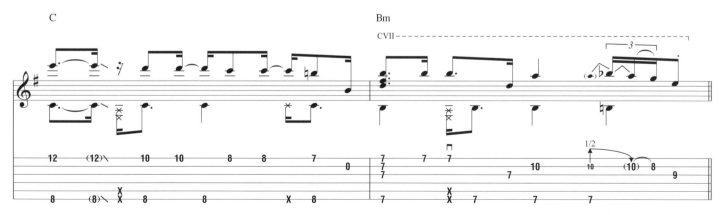

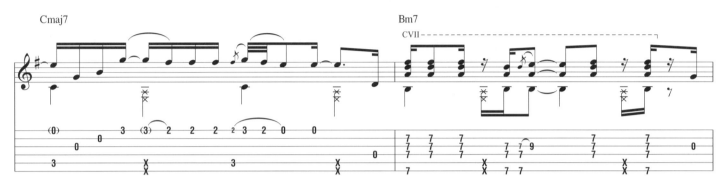

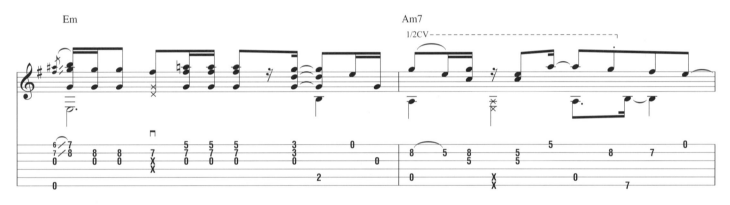

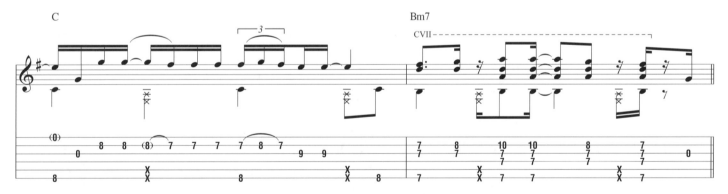

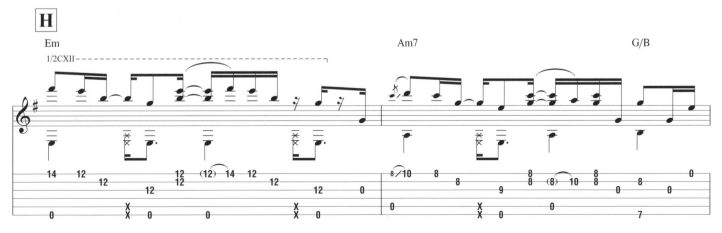

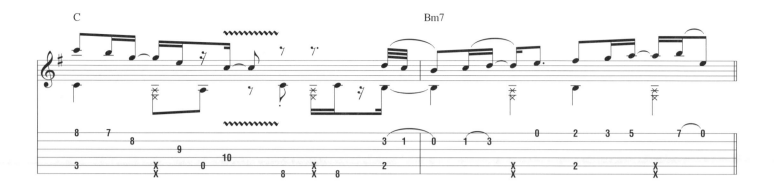

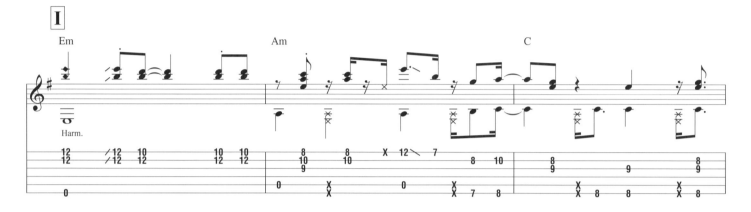

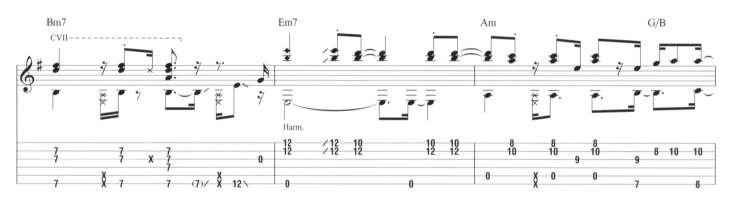

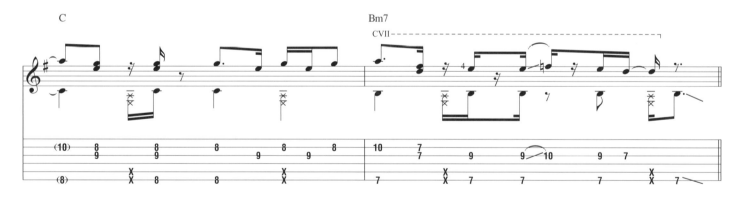

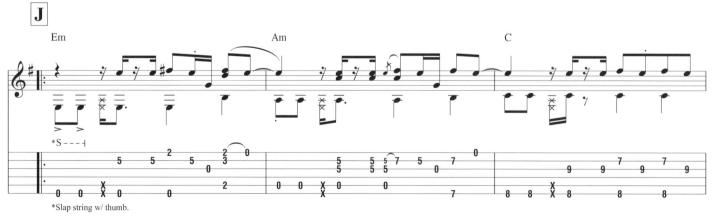

*Slap string w/ thumb.

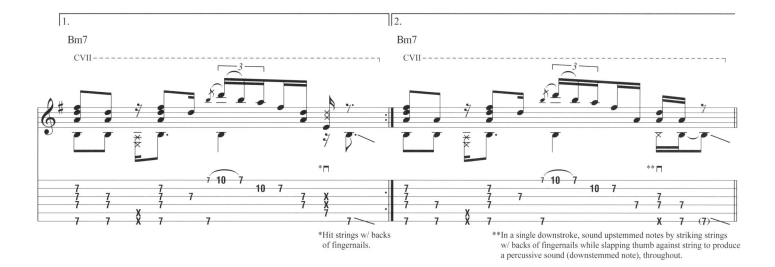

*Hit strings w/ backs
of fingernails.

**In a single downstroke, sound upstemmed notes by striking strings
w/ backs of fingernails while slapping thumb against string to produce
a percussive sound (downstemmed note), throughout.

K

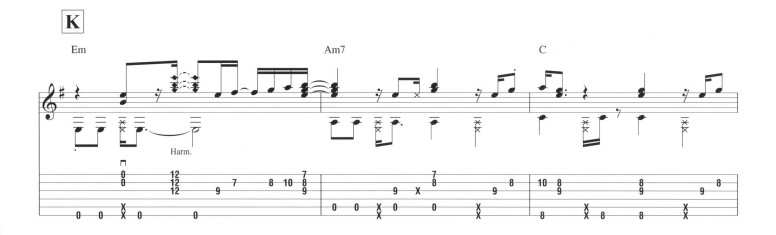

Harm.

***Strum as if holding a pick.

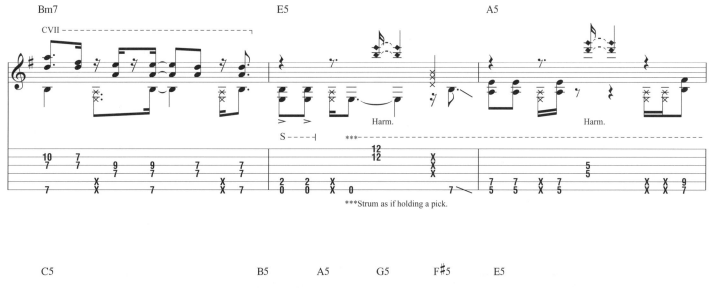

†Hit body of gtr.

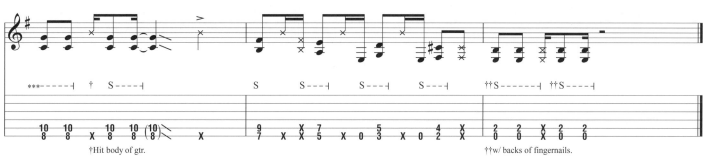

††w/ backs of fingernails.

Fade to Black

Words and Music by James Hetfield, Lars Ulrich, Cliff Burton and Kirk Hammett

Tune down 1 step:
(low to high) D-G-C-F-A-D

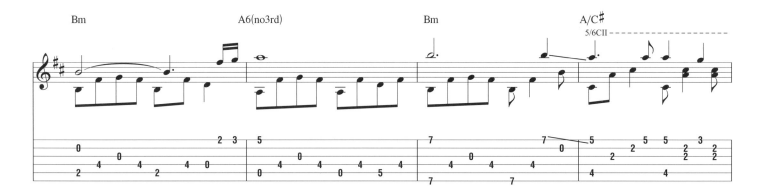

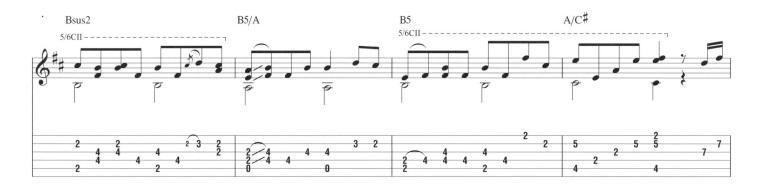

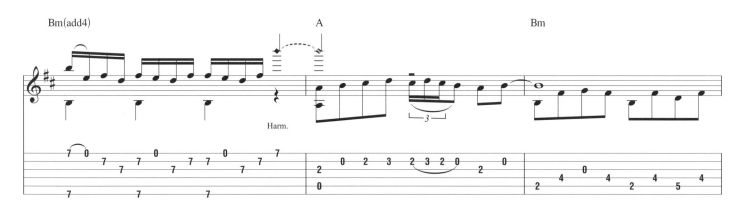

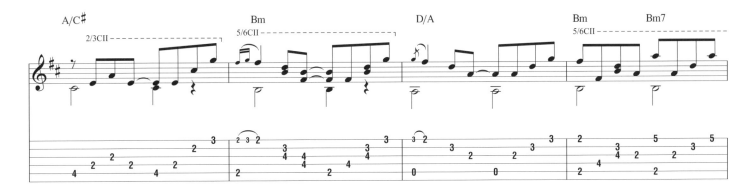

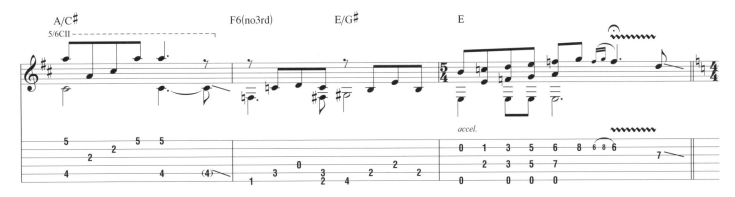

*Hit strings w/ back of fingernails.

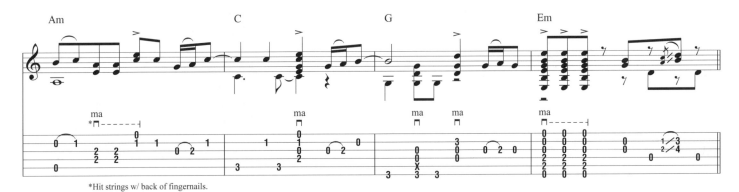

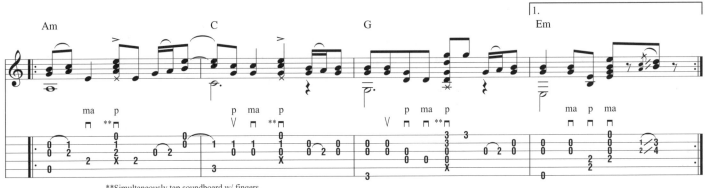

**Simultaneously tap soundboard w/ fingers
while strumming down w/ thumb (golpe).

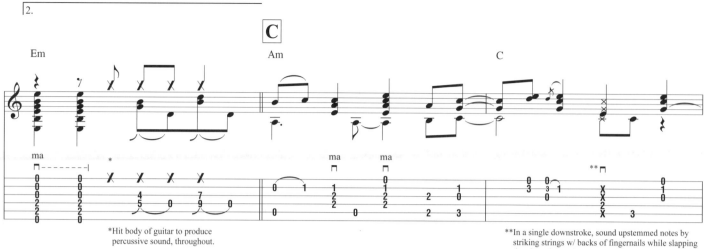

*Hit body of guitar to produce
percussive sound, throughout.

**In a single downstroke, sound upstemmed notes by
striking strings w/ backs of fingernails while slapping
thumb against strings to produce a percussive sound
(downstemmed notes), throughout.

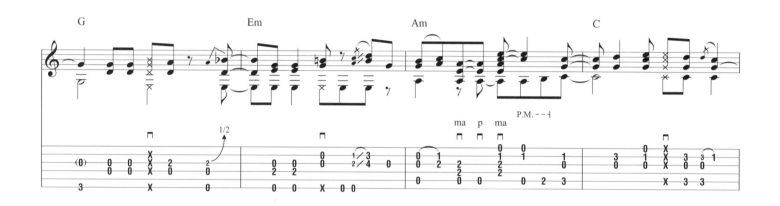

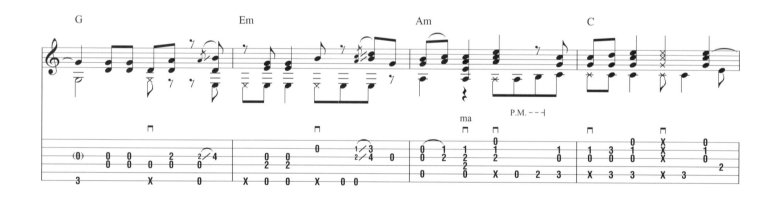

*Rasgueado (ami), throughout.

**Strum sim. except where indicated, next 15 meas.

***S=Slap strings w/ thumb.   †Hit body of guitar, as before.

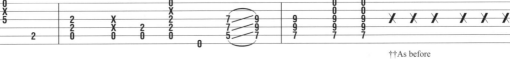

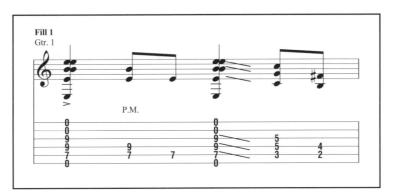

††As before

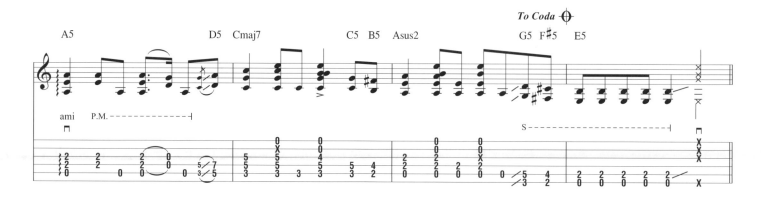

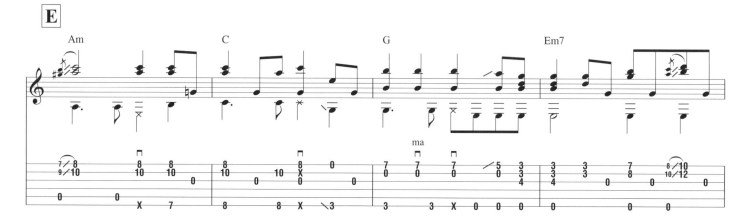

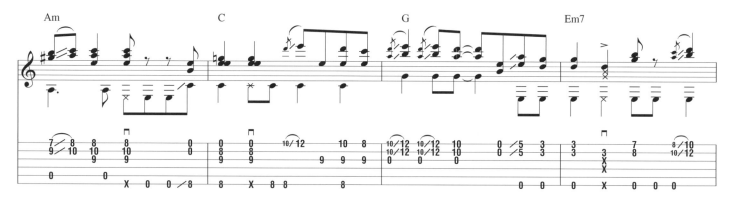

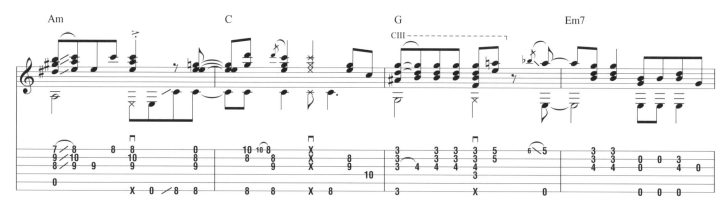

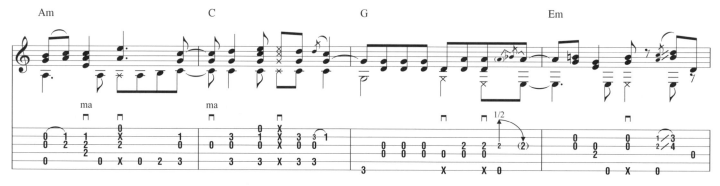

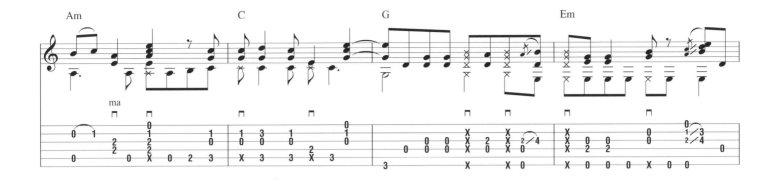

D.S. al Coda

Coda

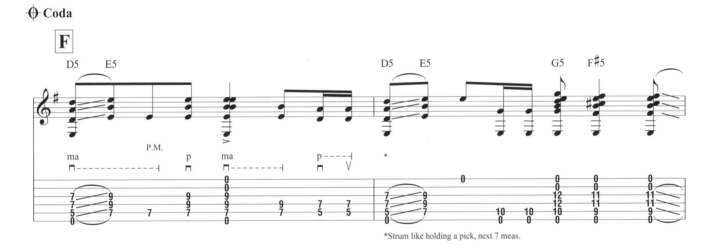

*Strum like holding a pick, next 7 meas.

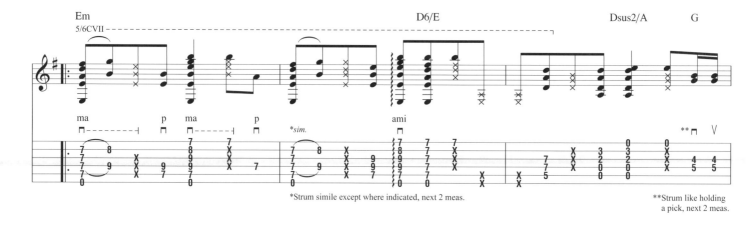

*Strum simile except where indicated, next 2 meas.

**Strum like holding a pick, next 2 meas.

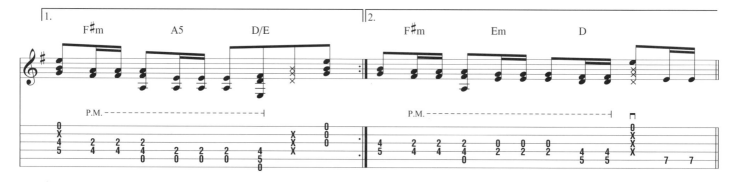

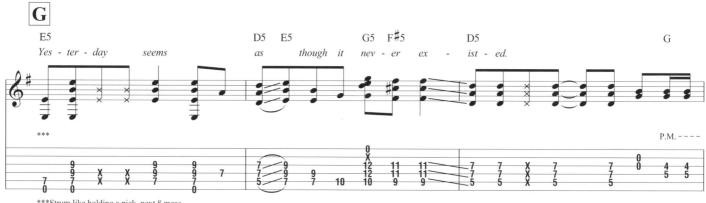

***Strum like holding a pick, next 8 meas.

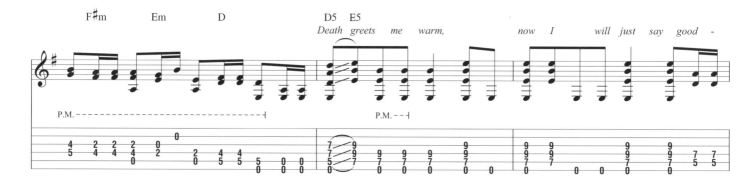

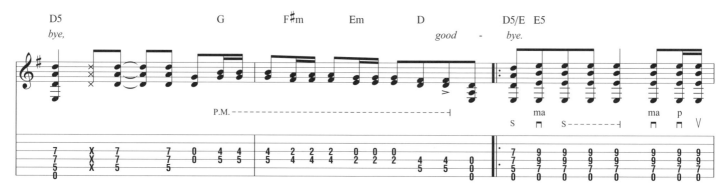

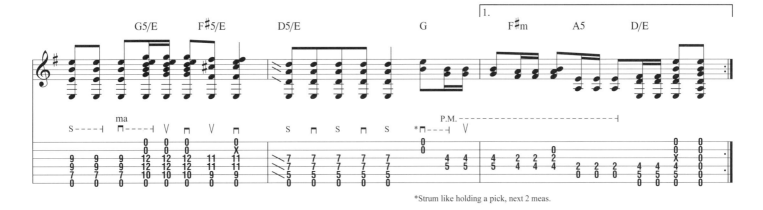

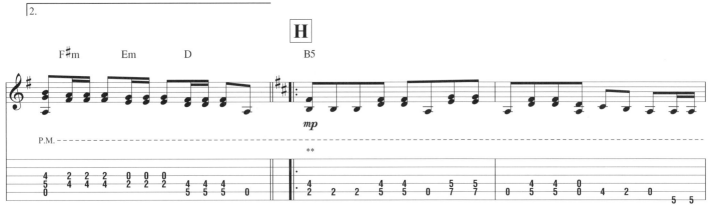

*Strum like holding a pick, next 2 meas.

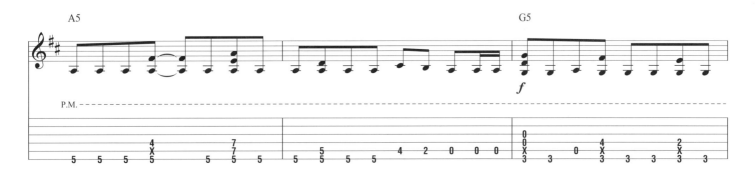

**Cont. strumming like holding a pick, next 16 meas.

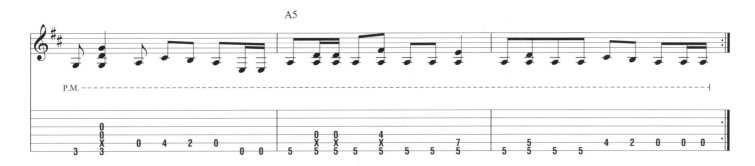

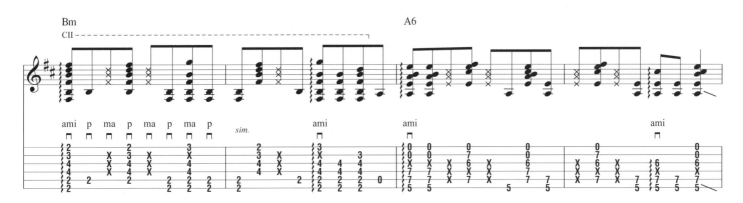

*Tap body of guitar w/ pick-hand fingers (top line of staff)
and thumb (2nd highest line of staff) in rhythm indicated.

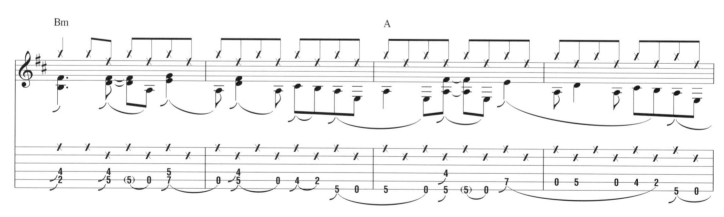

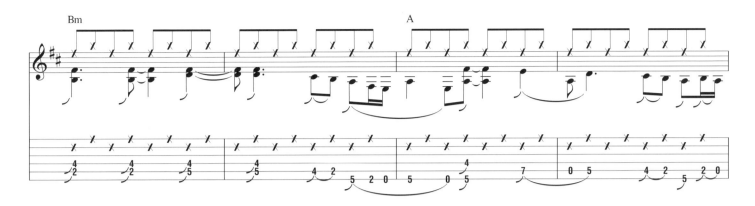

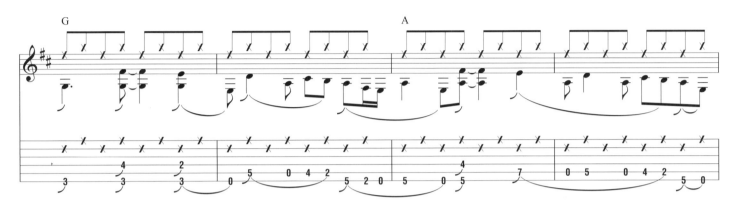

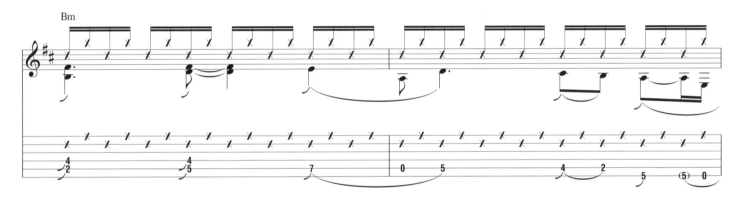

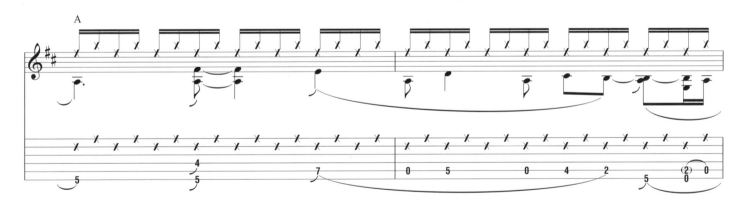

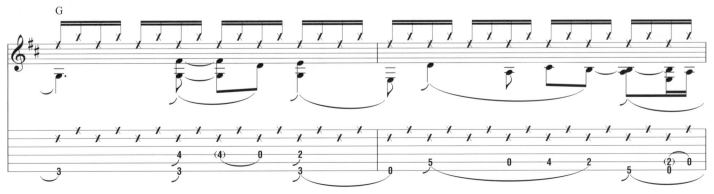

*Alternate between fingers and thumb
on body of guitar, simulating drum roll.

J

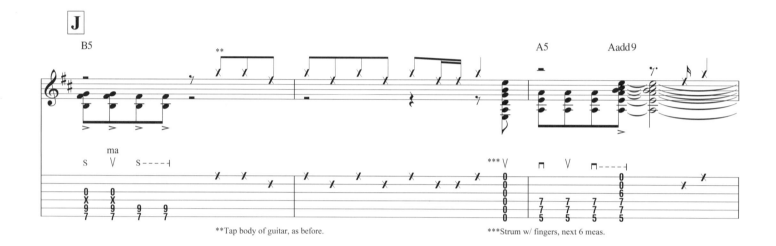

**Tap body of guitar, as before.

***Strum w/ fingers, next 6 meas.

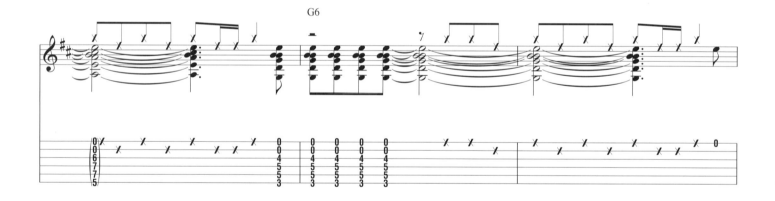

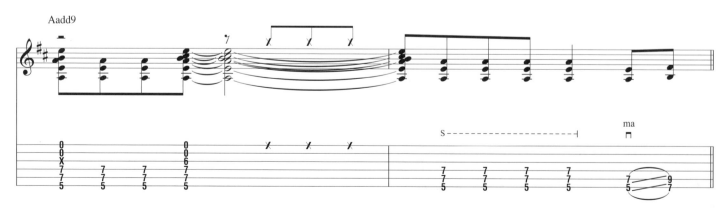

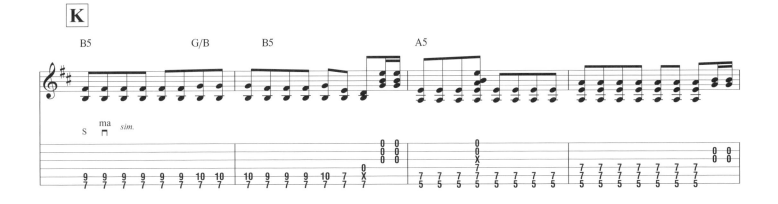

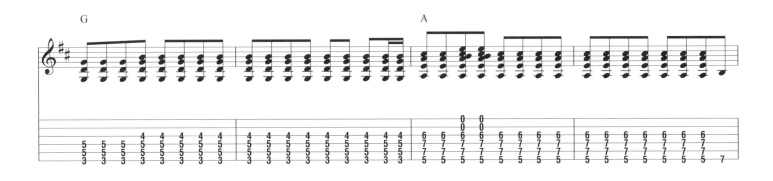

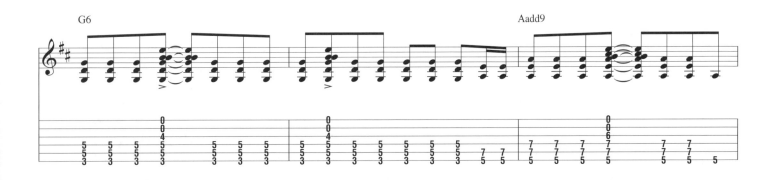

I Don't Want to Miss a Thing

from the Touchstone Picture ARMAGEDDON

Words and Music by Diane Warren

Open D tuning:
(low to high) D-A-D-F♯-A-D

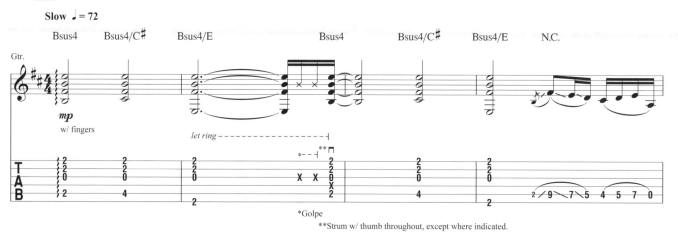

*Golpe

**Strum w/ thumb throughout, except where indicated.

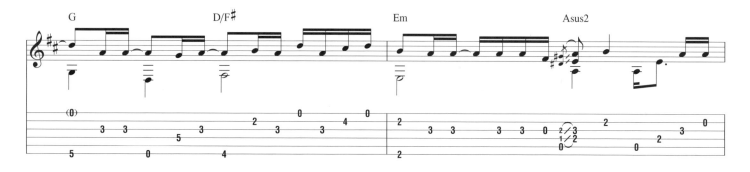

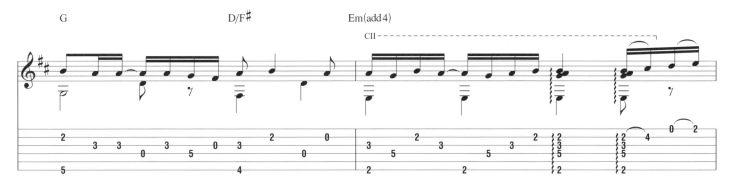

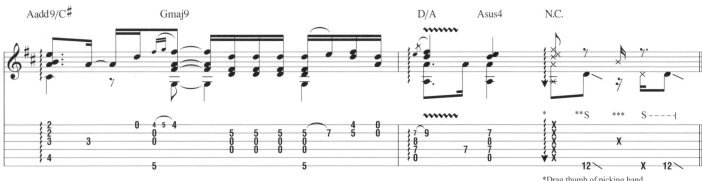

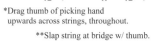

*Drag thumb of picking hand
upwards across strings, throughout.

**Slap string at bridge w/ thumb.

***Hit body of gtr.

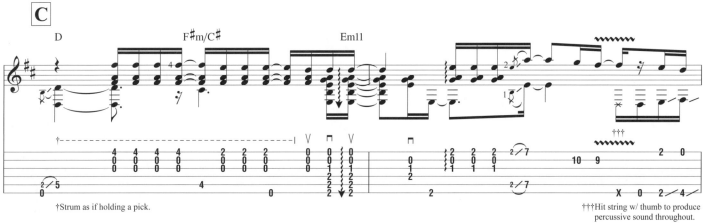

†Strum as if holding a pick.

†††Hit string w/ thumb to produce
percussive sound throughout.

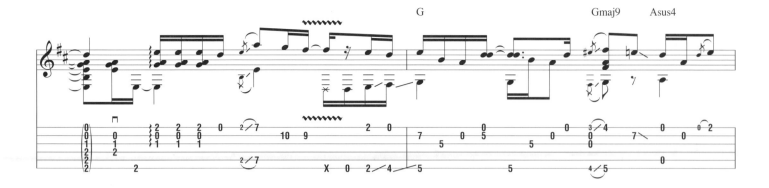

G   Gmaj9   Asus4

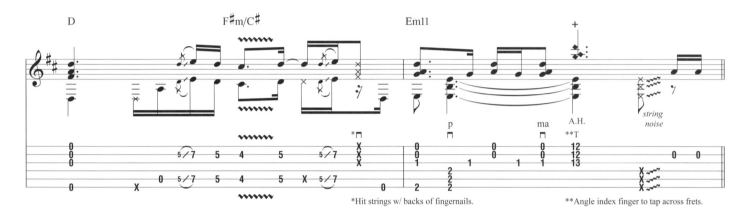

D   F#m/C#   Em11

*Hit strings w/ backs of fingernails.   **Angle index finger to tap across frets.

D

D   F#m/C#   Bm7

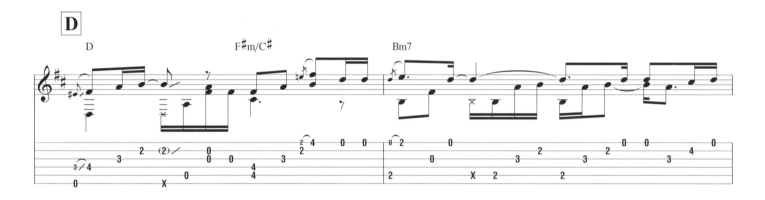

G   D/F#   Em   G/A

***In a single downstroke, sound upstemmed notes by striking strings w/ backs of fingernails while
slapping thumb against strings to produce a percussive sound (downstemmed notes), throughout.

D   F#m/C#   Bm7

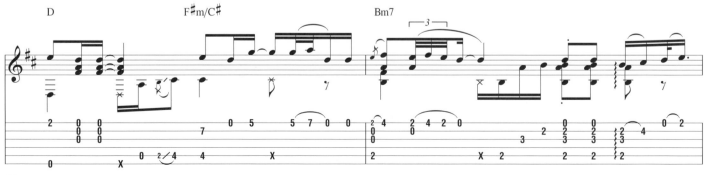

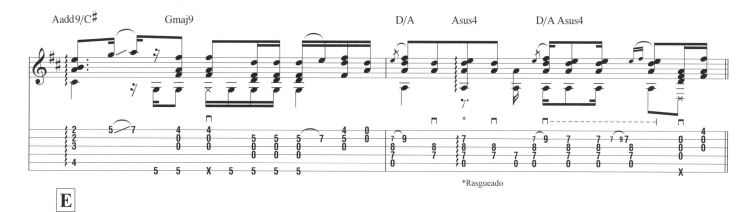

Aadd9/C#   Gmaj9   D/A   Asus4   D/A Asus4

*Rasgueado

E

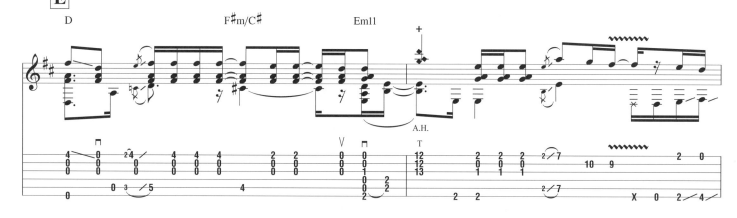

D   F#m/C#   Em11

A.H.

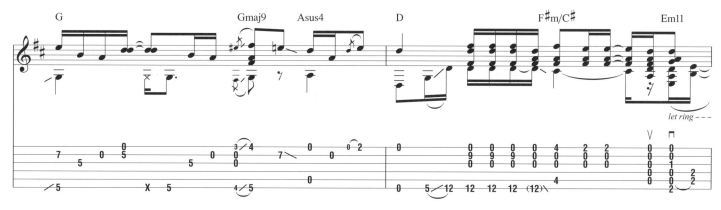

G   Gmaj9   Asus4   D   F#m/C#   Em11

let ring - - -

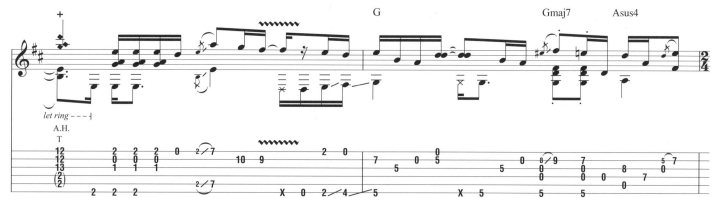

let ring - - -

A.H.

                                    G   Gmaj7   Asus4

F

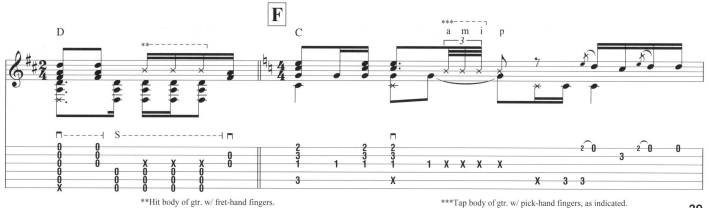

D   C   a   m   i   p

**Hit body of gtr. w/ fret-hand fingers.   ***Tap body of gtr. w/ pick-hand fingers, as indicated.

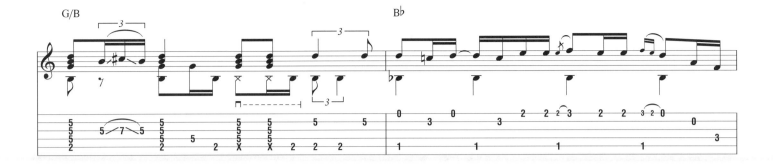

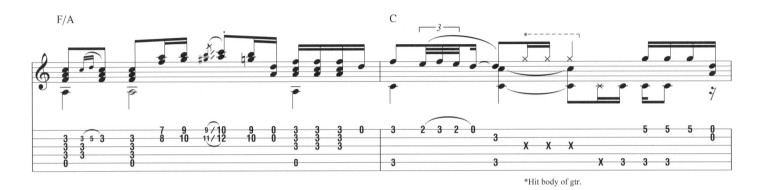

*Hit body of gtr.

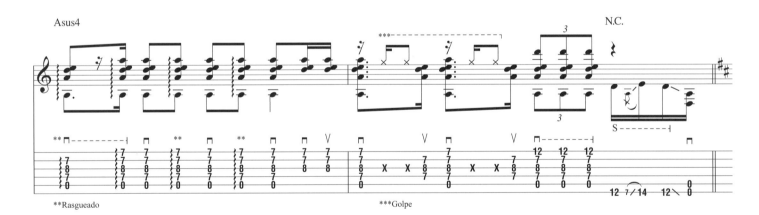

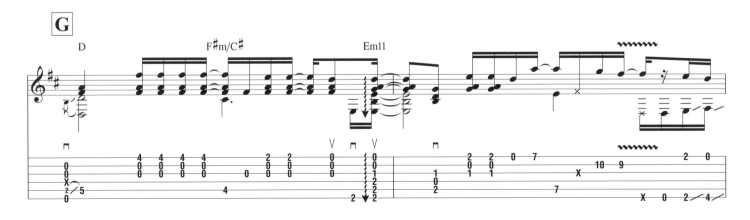

**Rasgueado   ***Golpe

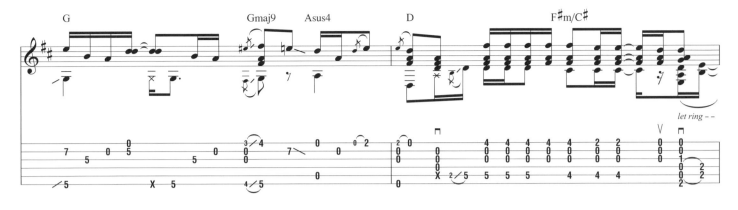

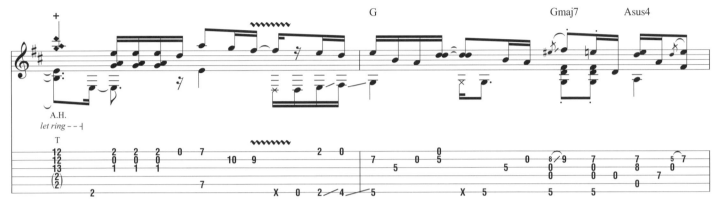

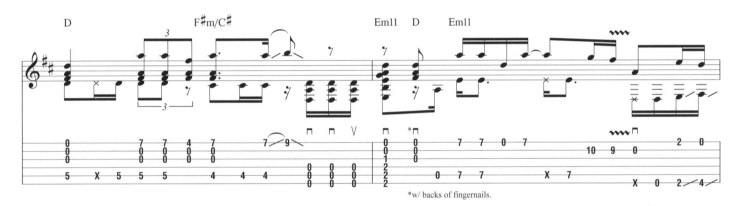

*w/ backs of fingernails.

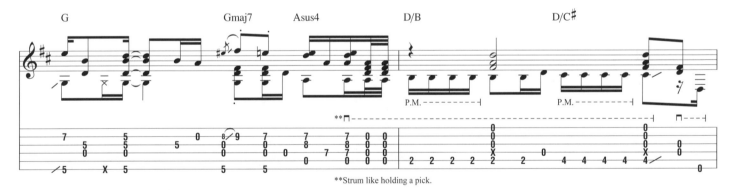

**Strum like holding a pick.

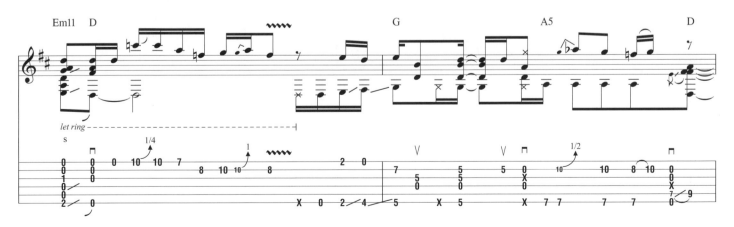

*Single downstroke
w/ thumb slap, as before.

And I don't want to miss a thing.

**Strum like holding a pick.

***Hit body of gtr.

†Rasgueado

††Refers to top 2 strings only.

†††Strum like holding a pick.

‡Rasgueado

Money

Words and Music by Roger Waters

Tune down 1 step:
(low to high) D-G-C-F-A-D

*Chord symbols reflect implied harmony.

**Slap strings w/ thumb.
***Rasgueado

††Hit edge of palm across strings
to produce percussive sound.

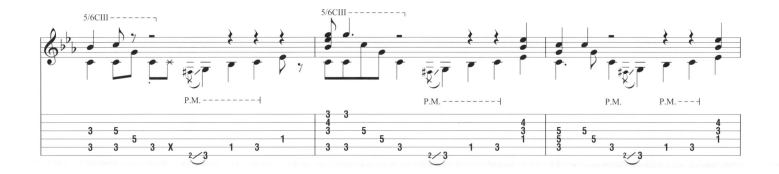

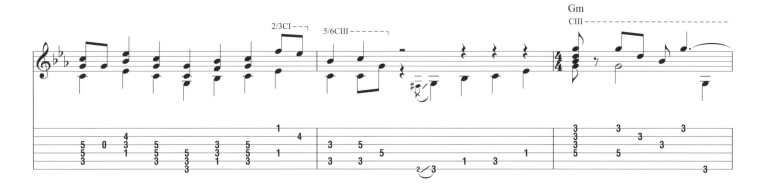

To Coda ⊕

C

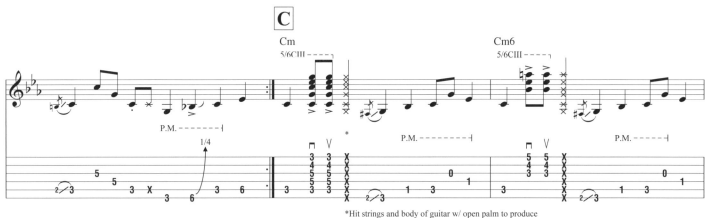

*Hit strings and body of guitar w/ open palm to produce
percussive sound, throughout, except where indicated.

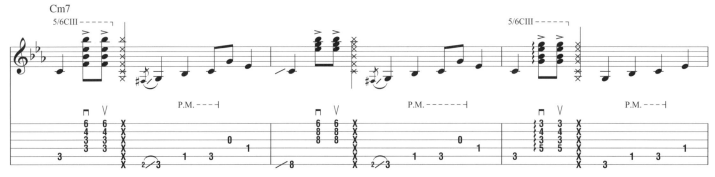

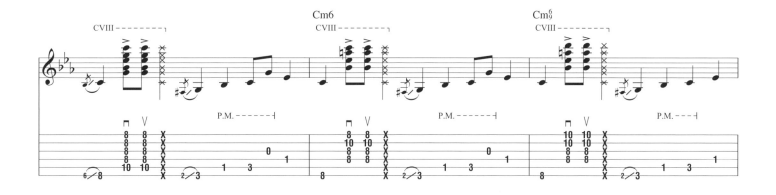

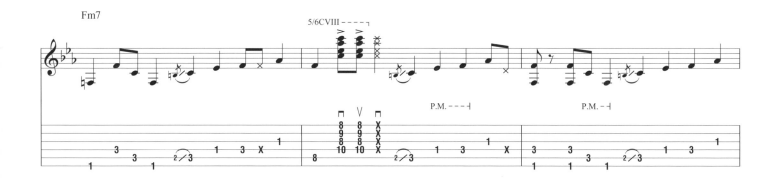

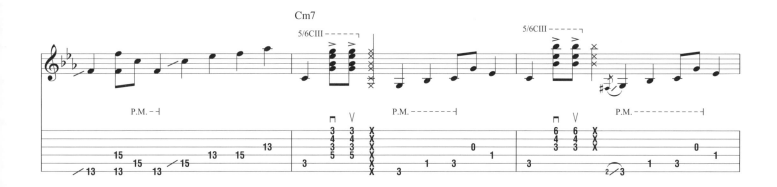

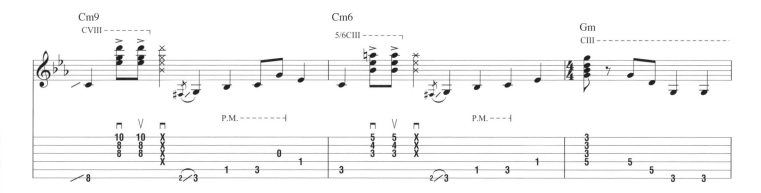

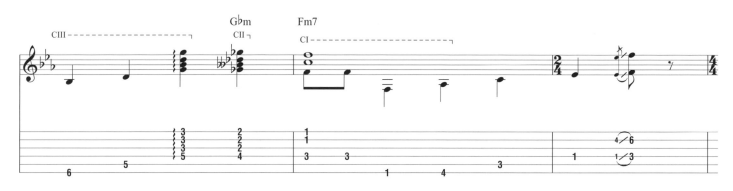

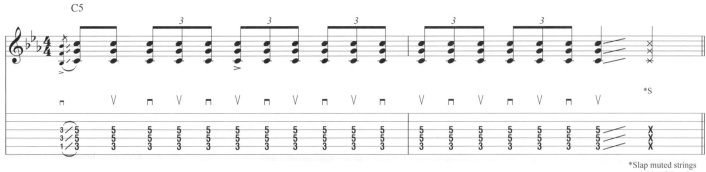

C5

*S

*Slap muted strings
w/ side of thumb.

D

Cm7

CIII - - - - - - -

CVIII - - - - - - - -

**P.M.

**P.M. on downstemmed notes, next 12 meas.

CVIII - - - - - - - - - -

CVIII - - - - - - - - - - - -

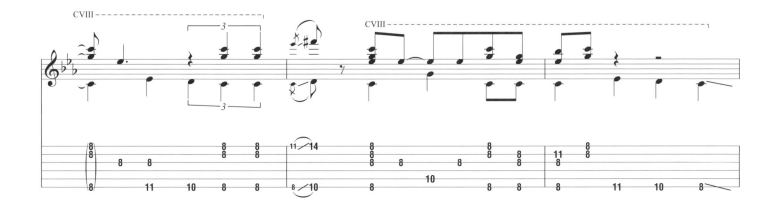

CIII -

Fm

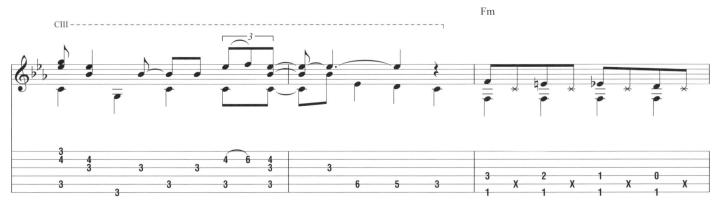

46

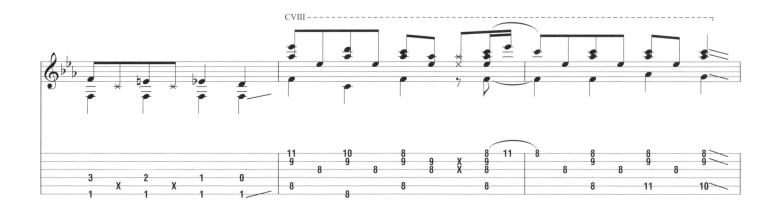

Cm7

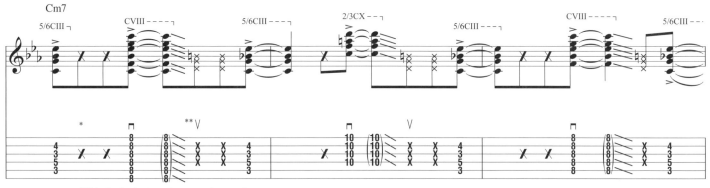

*Hit body of guitar to produce percussive sound, throughout, except where indicated.

**w/ backs of fingernails.

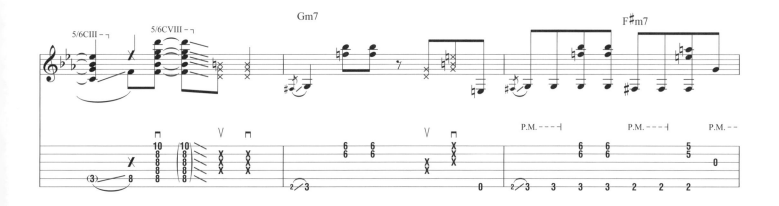

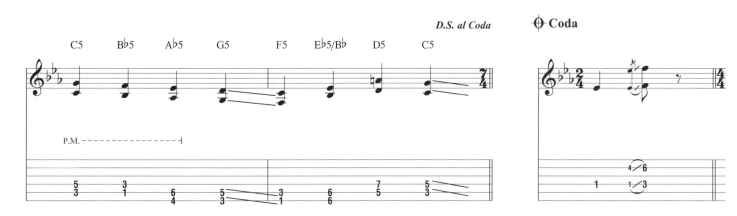

E

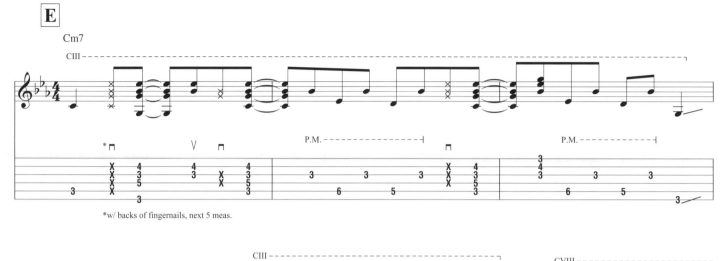

*w/ backs of fingernails, next 5 meas.

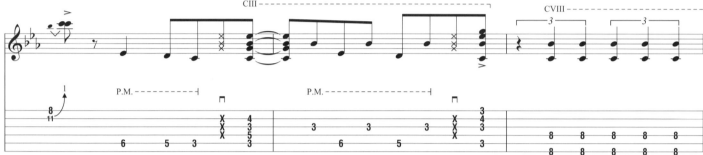

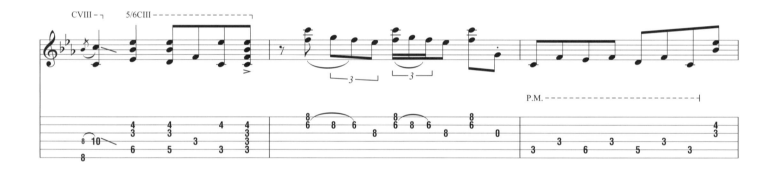

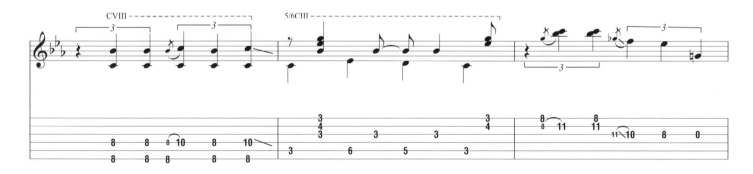

Free time

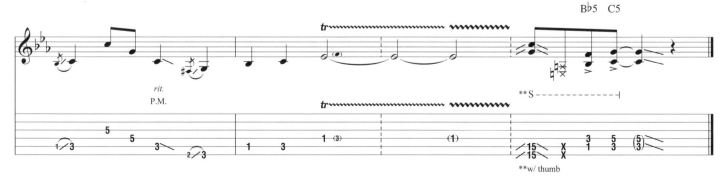

**S

**w/ thumb

More Than a Feeling

Words and Music by Tom Scholz

Tune down 1 step:
(low to high) D-G-C-F-A-D

*Harp harmonic achieved by touching string w/ pick-hand index finger
at fret indicated in parentheses and plucking w/ thumb.

**Slap w/ thumb.
***Hit string
w/ backs of
fingernails.

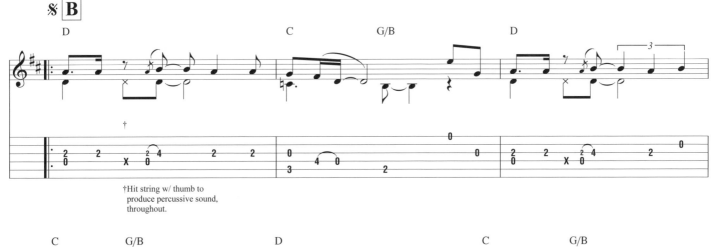

†Hit string w/ thumb to
produce percussive sound,
throughout.

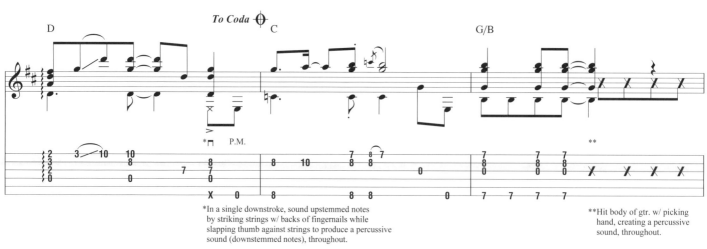

*In a single downstroke, sound upstemmed notes
by striking strings w/ backs of fingernails while
slapping thumb against strings to produce a percussive
sound (downstemmed notes), throughout.

**Hit body of gtr. w/ picking
hand, creating a percussive
sound, throughout.

***As before, except hit heel of palm on bridge
to produce deeper percussive sound, throughout.

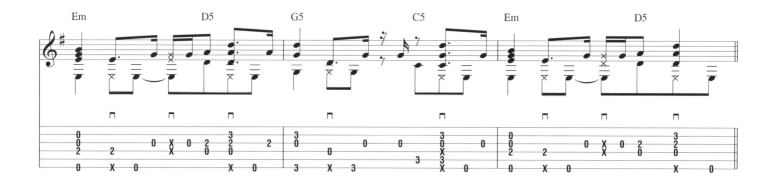

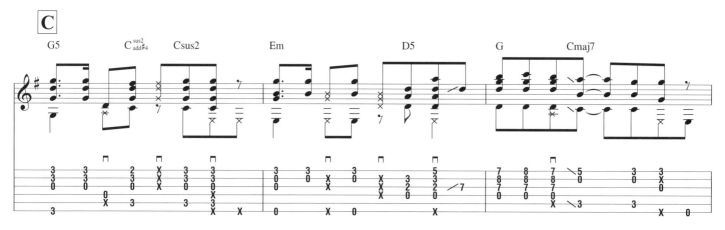

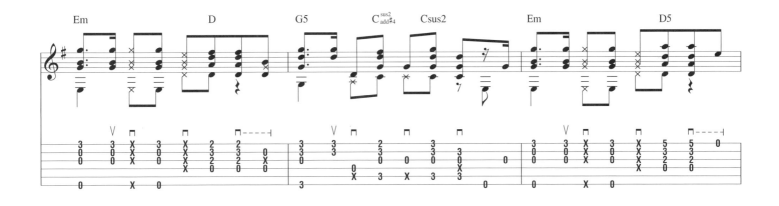

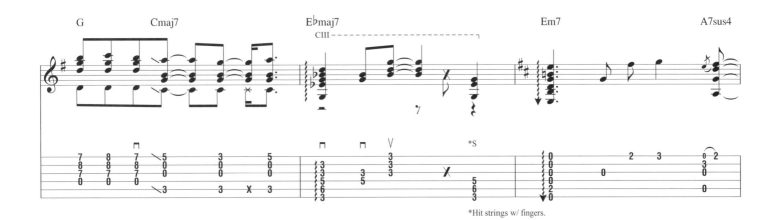

*Hit strings w/ fingers.

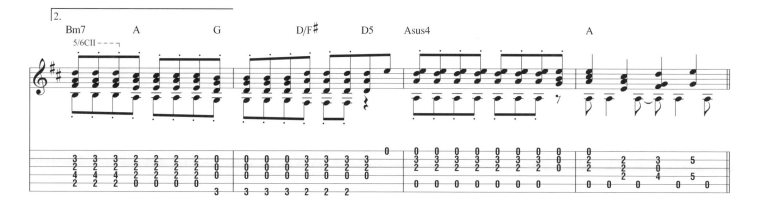

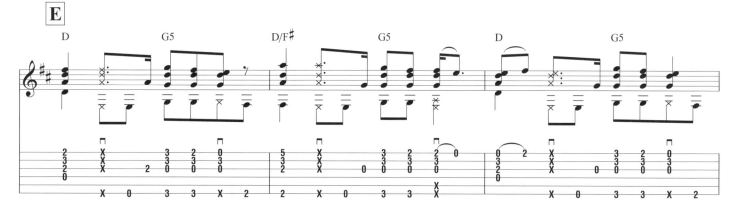

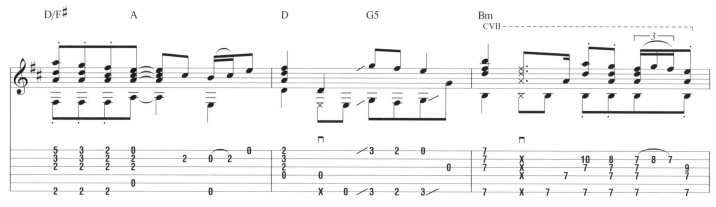

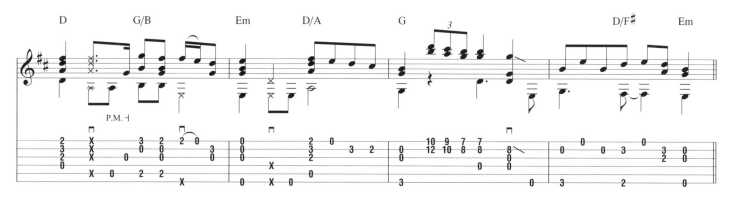

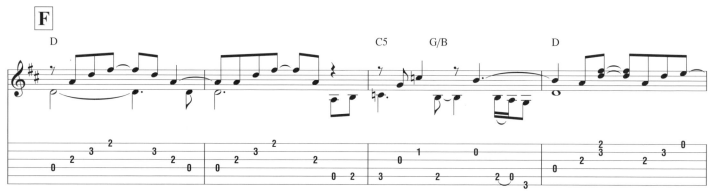

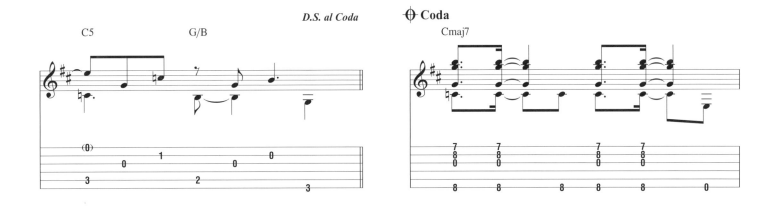

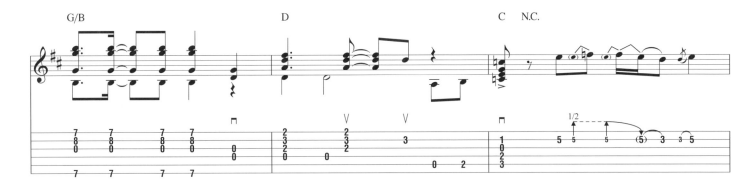

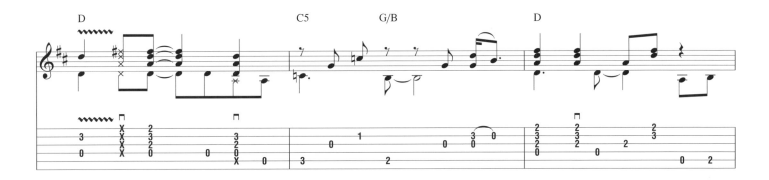

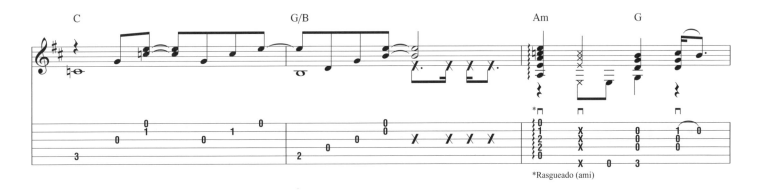

*Rasgueado (ami)

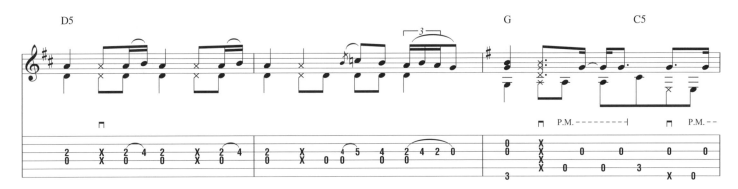

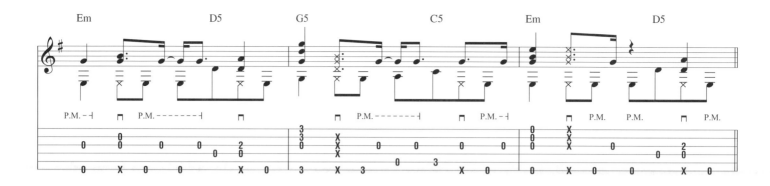

G

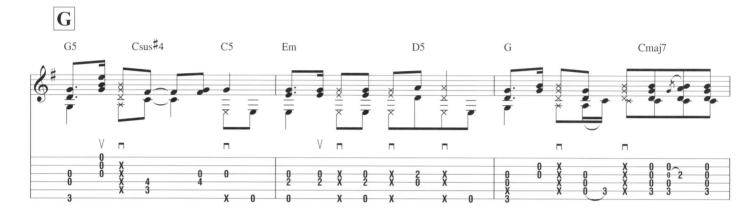

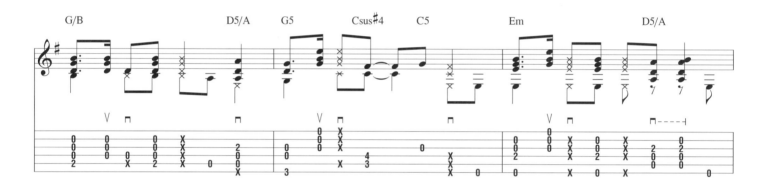

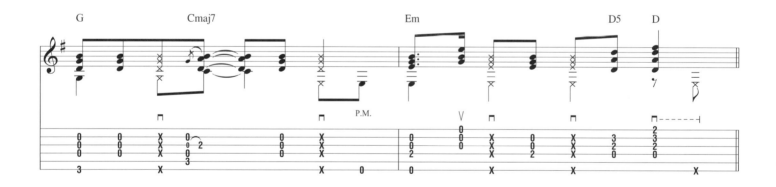

Play 6 times and fade

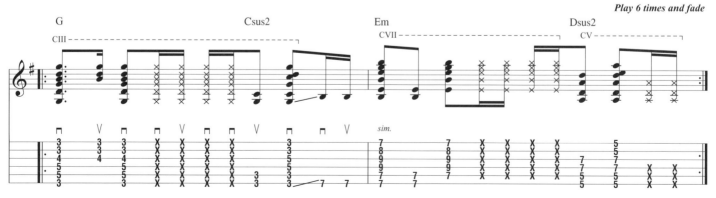

No Woman No Cry

Words and Music by Vincent Ford

Tune down 1 1/2 steps:
(low to high) C#-F#-B-E-G#-C#

*Hit strings w/ backs of fingernails.

**In a single downstroke, sound upstemmed notes by striking strings w/ backs of fingernails while slapping thumb against strings to produce a percussive sound (downstemmed notes), throughout.

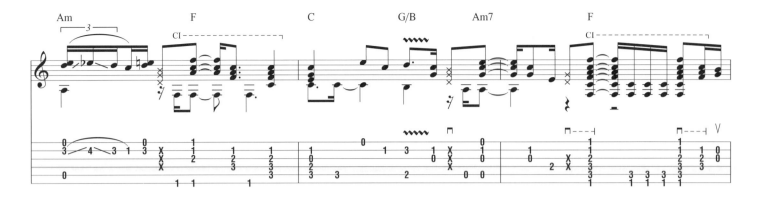

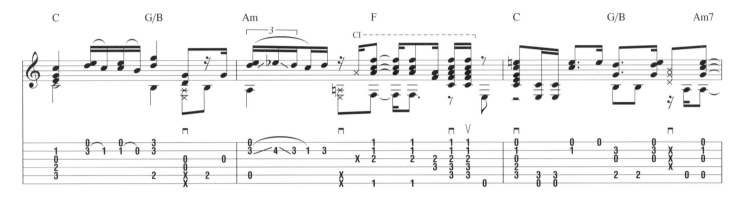

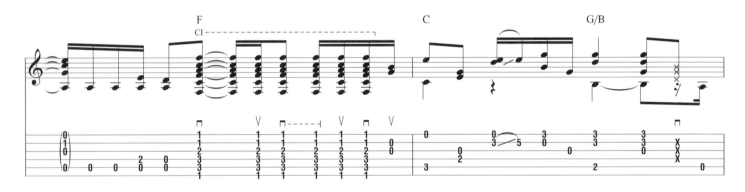

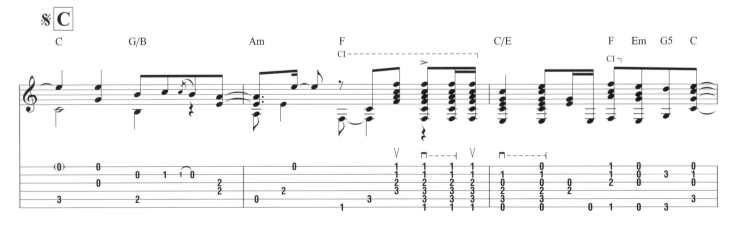

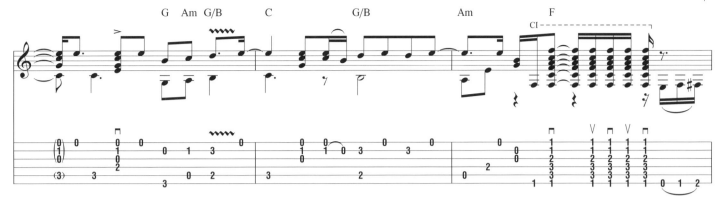

D

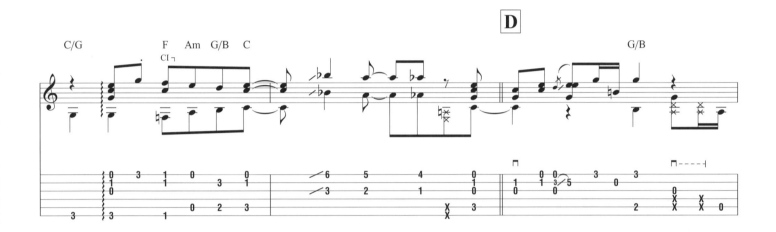

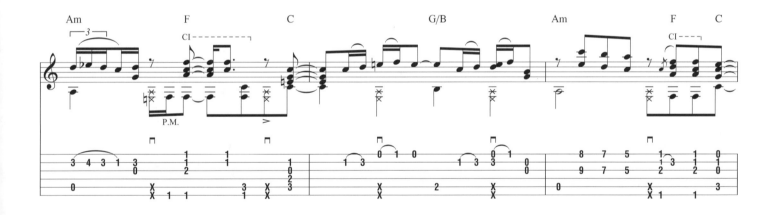

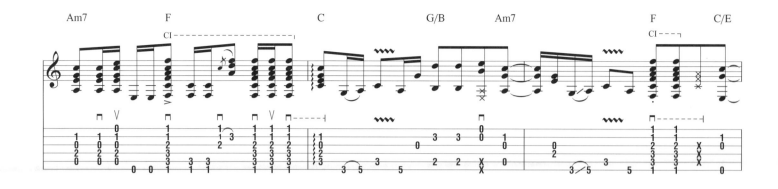

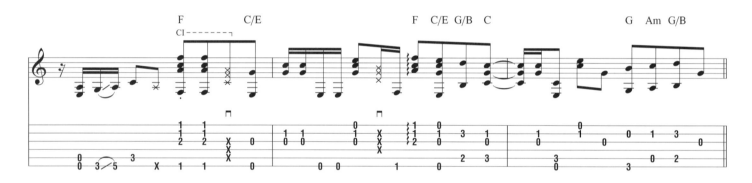

E

Sung: No woman no cry.

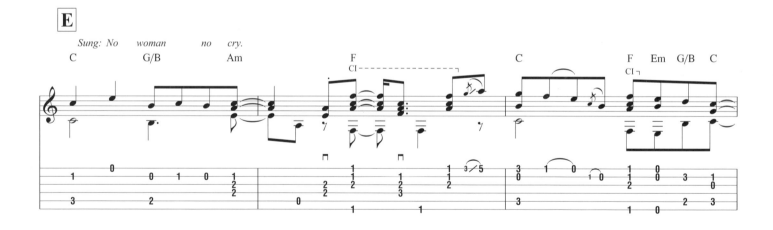

No woman no cry, *oh, no*

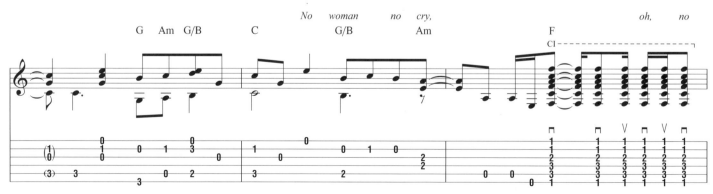

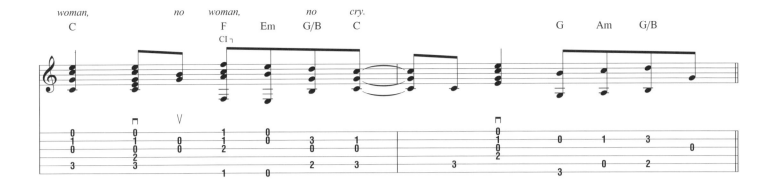

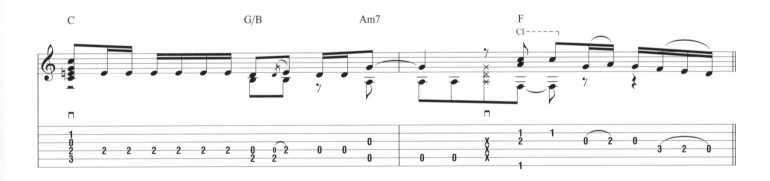

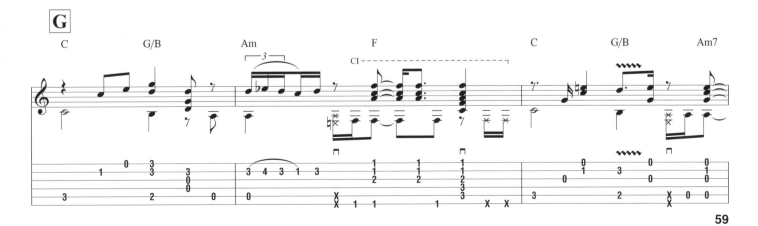

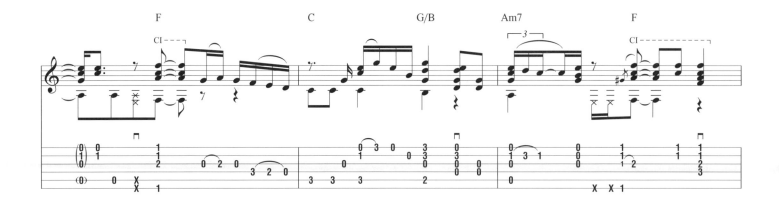

D.S. al Coda

⊕ **Coda**

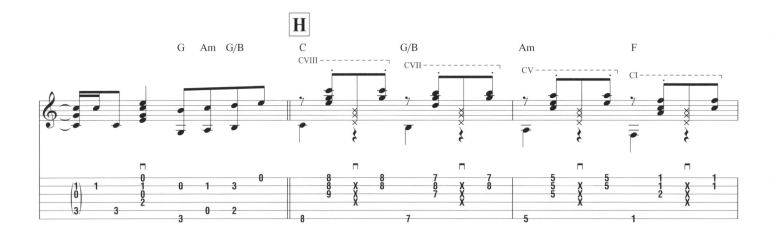

H

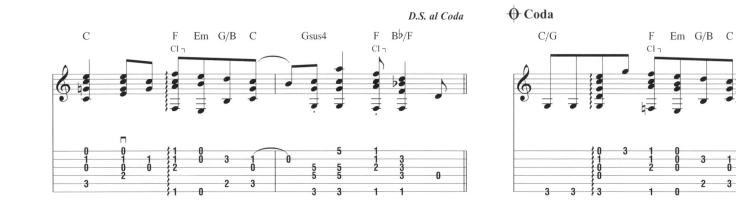

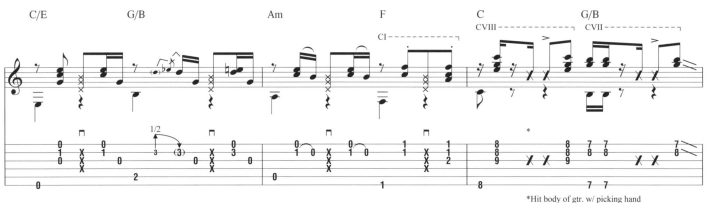

*Hit body of gtr. w/ picking hand
creating a percussive sound, throughout.

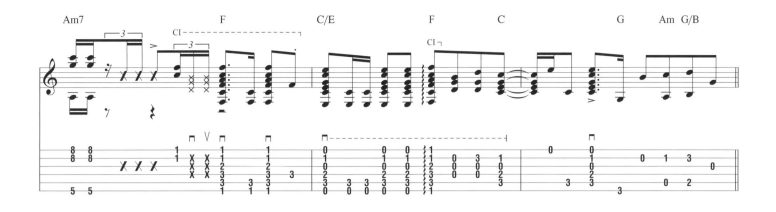

I

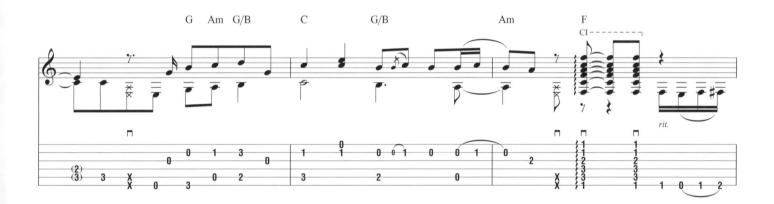

Free time

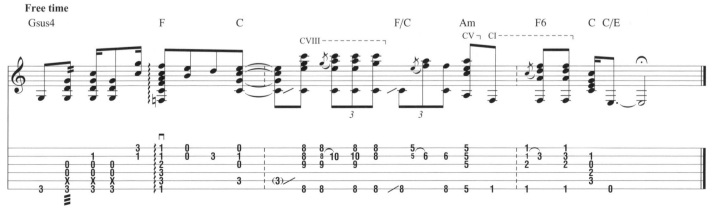

November Rain

Words and Music by W. Axl Rose

Drop C tuning, down 1 step:
(low to high) B♭-G-C-F-A-D

A

Moderately slow ♩ = 78

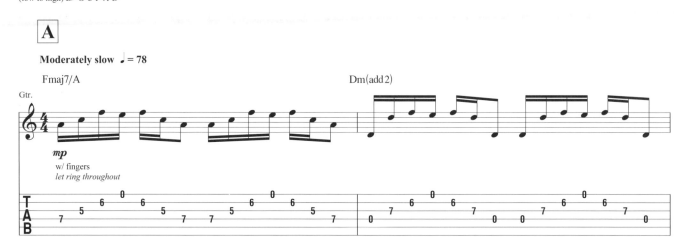

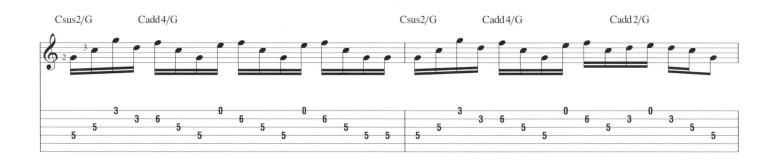

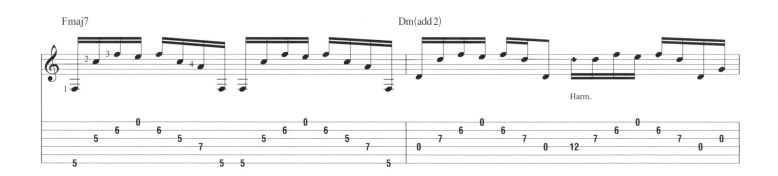

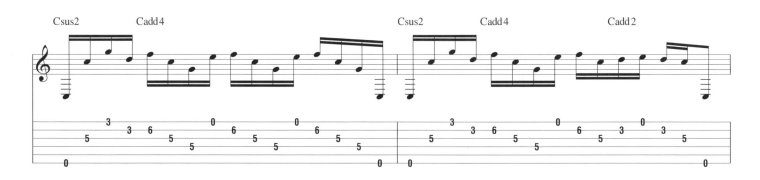

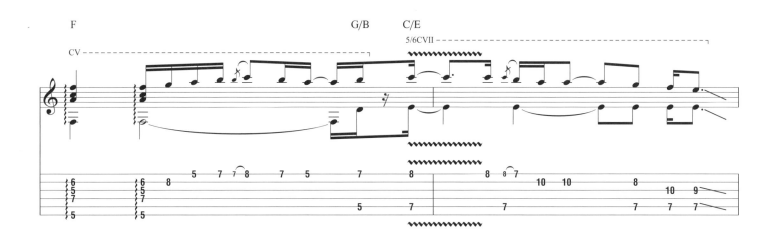

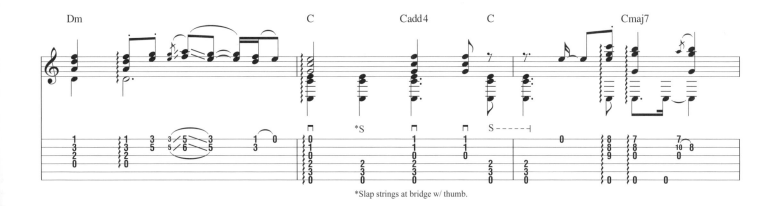

*Slap strings at bridge w/ thumb.

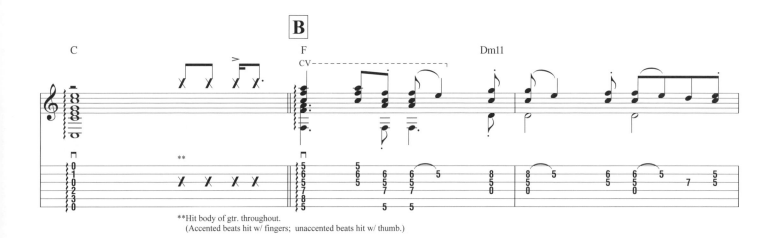

**Hit body of gtr. throughout.
(Accented beats hit w/ fingers; unaccented beats hit w/ thumb.)

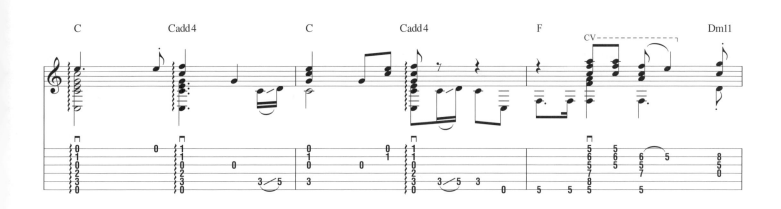

*Tap sound board w/ finger tips.

**Rasgueado (ami) throughout

***Strum like holding a pick.

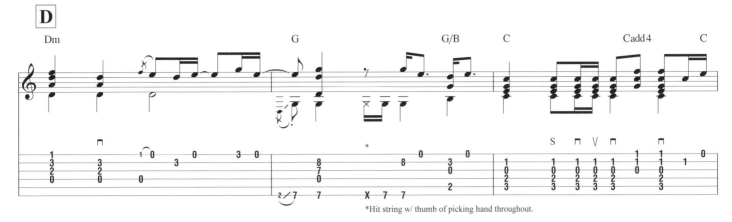

*Hit string w/ thumb of picking hand throughout.

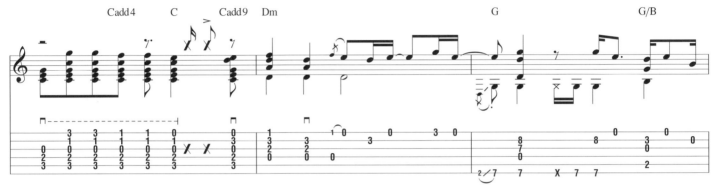

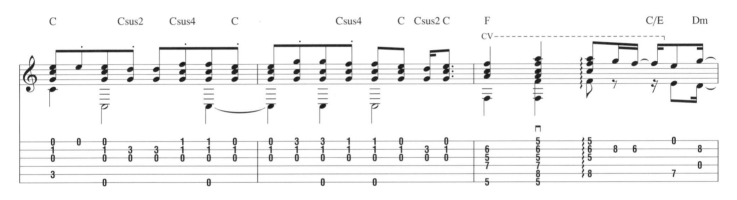

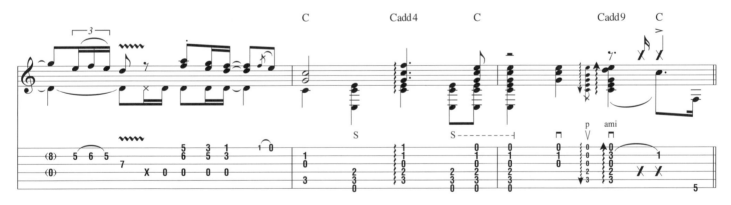

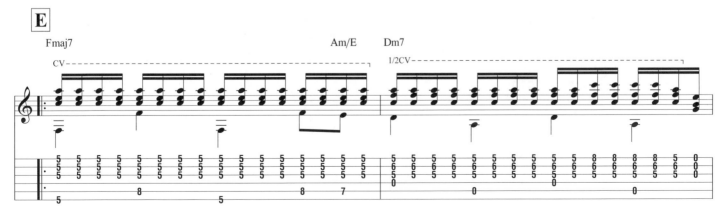

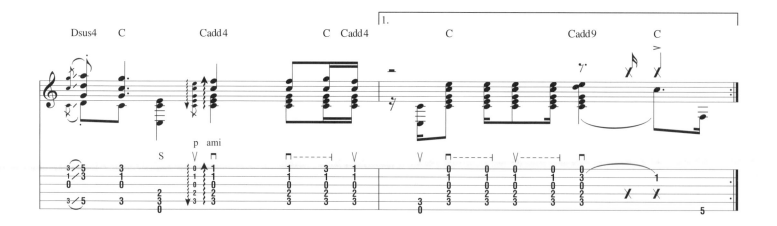

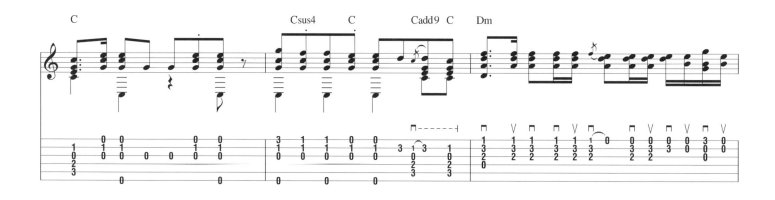

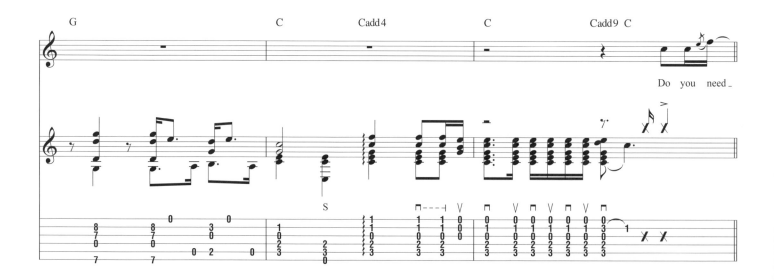

Do you need

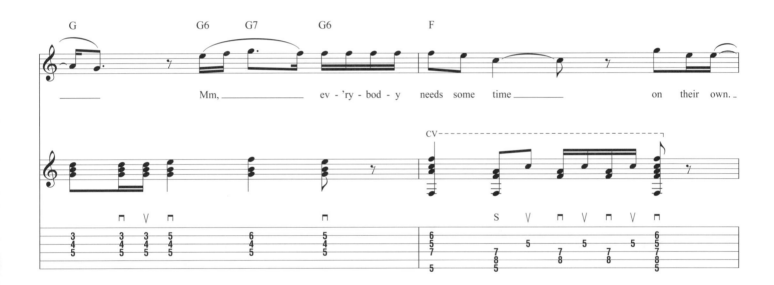

I know it's hard to keep an o - pen heart when e-ven friends seem out to harm

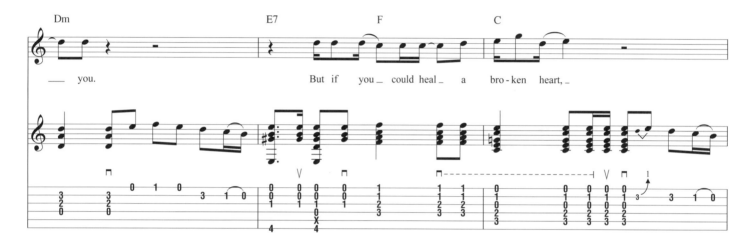

you. But if you could heal a bro - ken heart,

would-n't time be out to charm you? Whoa, oh, oh.

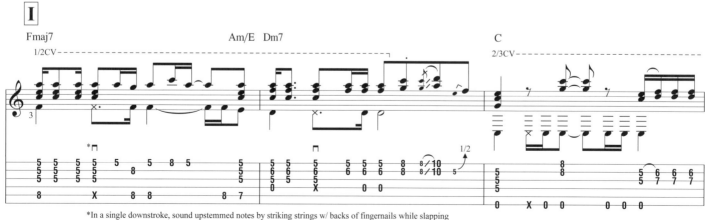

*In a single downstroke, sound upstemmed notes by striking strings w/ backs of fingernails while slapping thumb against lower string to produce a percussive sound (downstemmed notes) throughout.

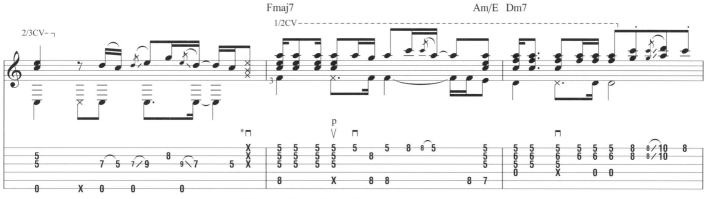

*Hit strings w/ backs of fingernails to produce a percussive sound.

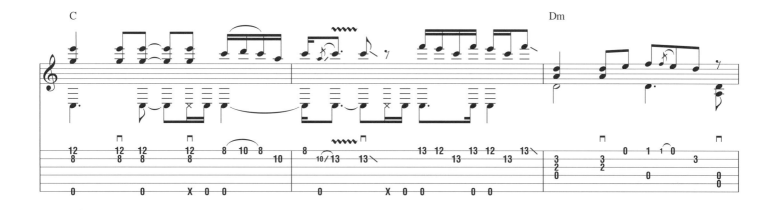

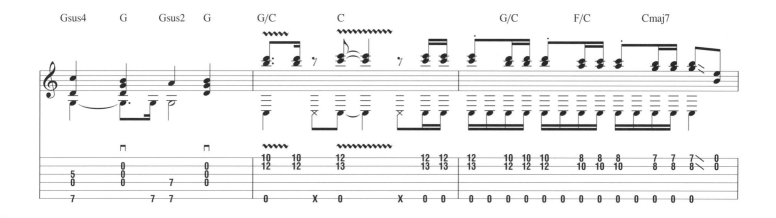

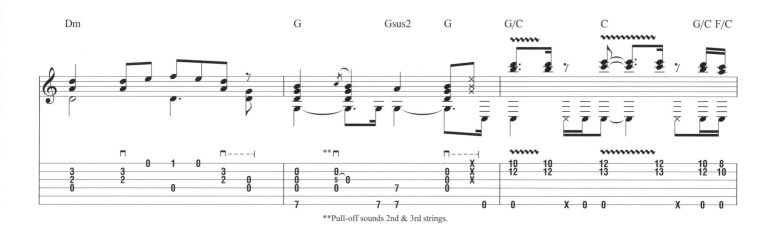

**Pull-off sounds 2nd & 3rd strings.

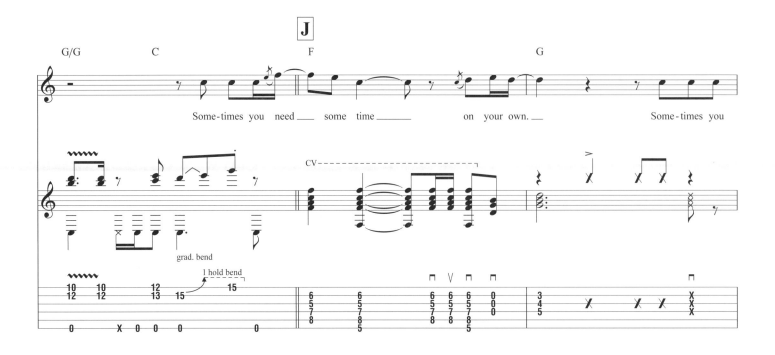

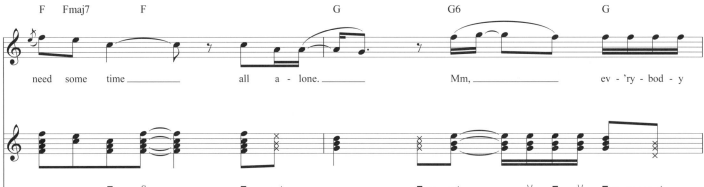

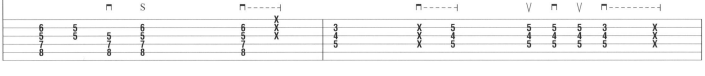

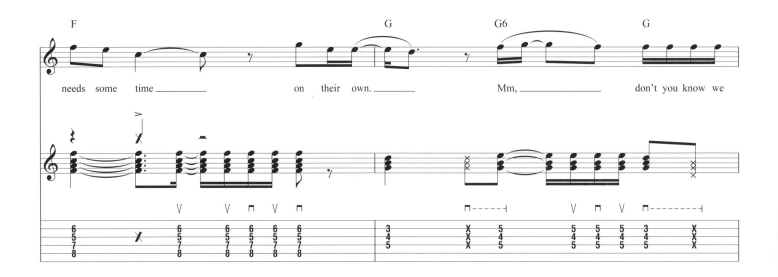

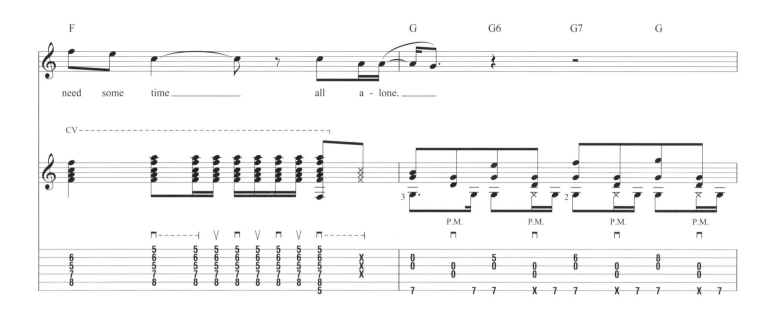

need   some   time _____   all   a - lone. _____

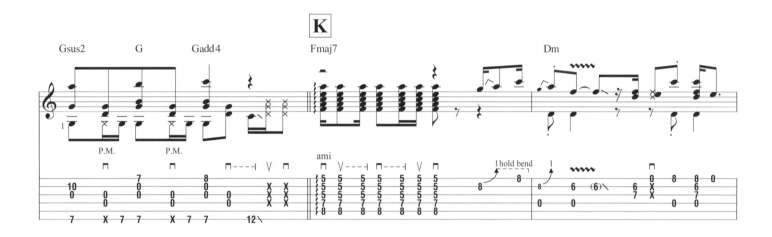

K

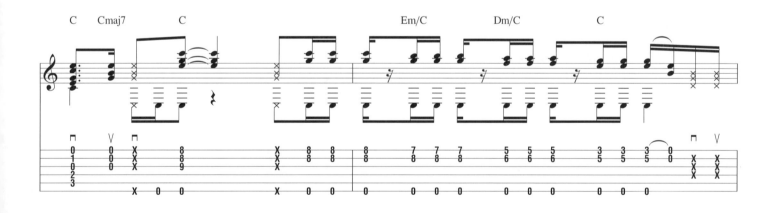

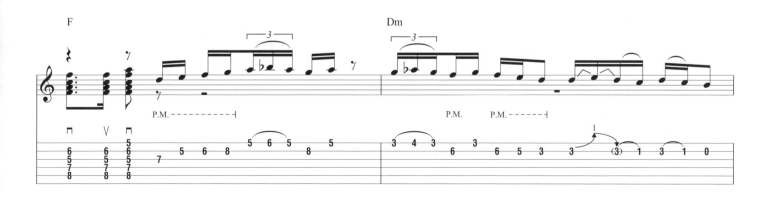

L

When your fears _ sub - side _ and shad - ows _ still re - main, _ mm, _

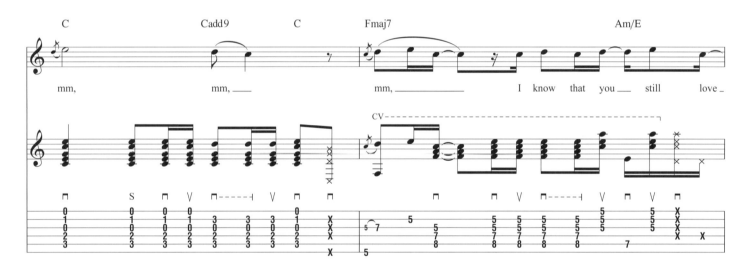

mm, _ mm, _ mm, _ I know that you _ still love _

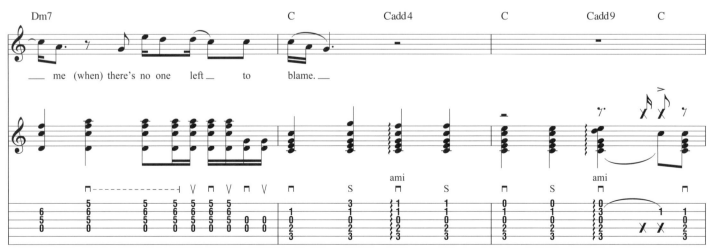

_ me (when) there's no one left _ to blame. _

*Strum like holding a pick, next 7 meas.

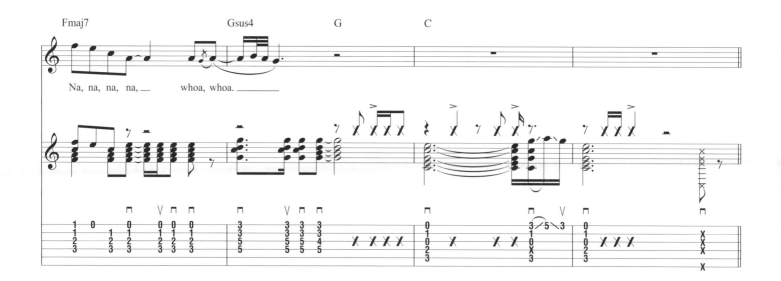

Na, na, na, na, __ whoa, whoa. __

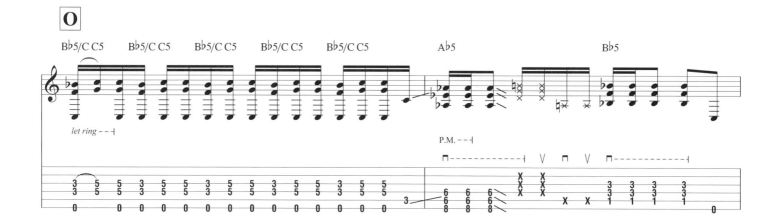

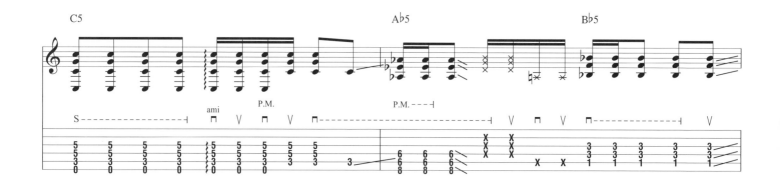

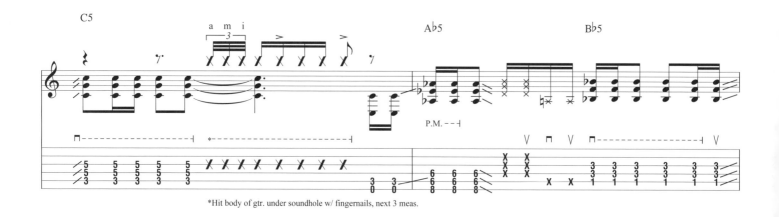

*Hit body of gtr. under soundhole w/ fingernails, next 3 meas.

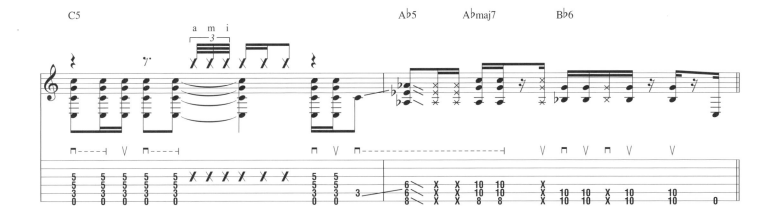

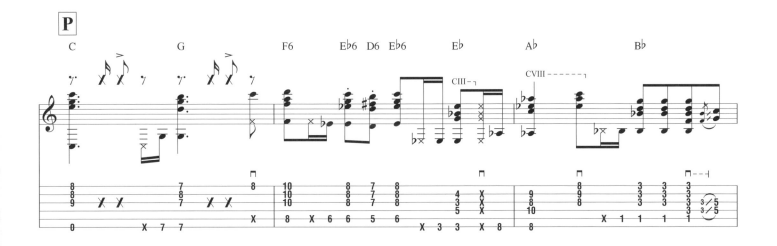

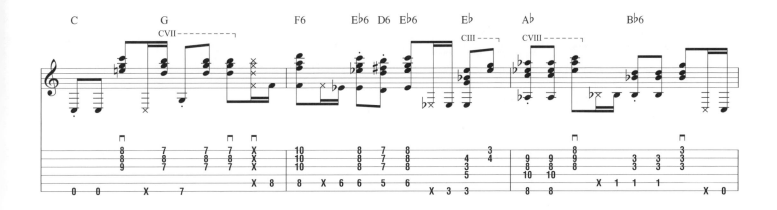

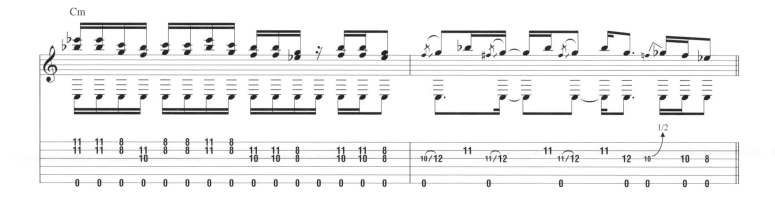

Q

Don't you think that you need some-bod-y? Don't you think that you need some - one?

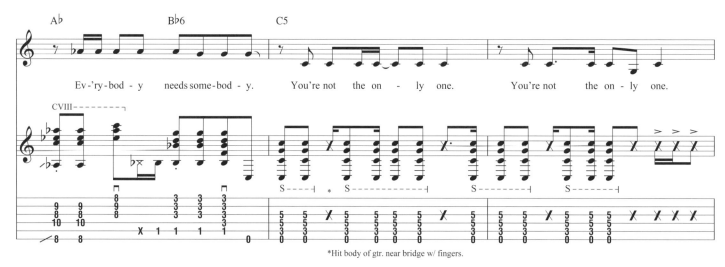

Ev-'ry-bod - y needs some-bod-y. You're not the on - ly one. You're not the on - ly one.

*Hit body of gtr. near bridge w/ fingers.

Don't you think that you need some-bod - y? Don't you think that you need some - one?

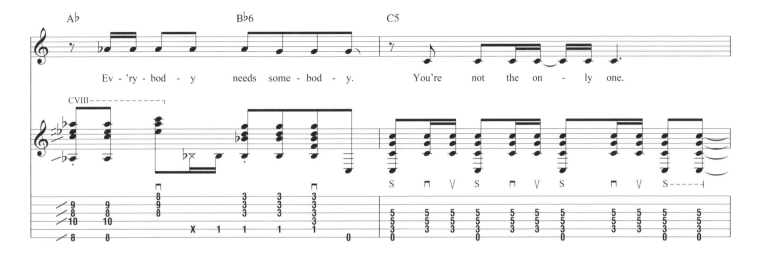

Ev - 'ry - bod - y needs some - bod - y. You're not the on - ly one.

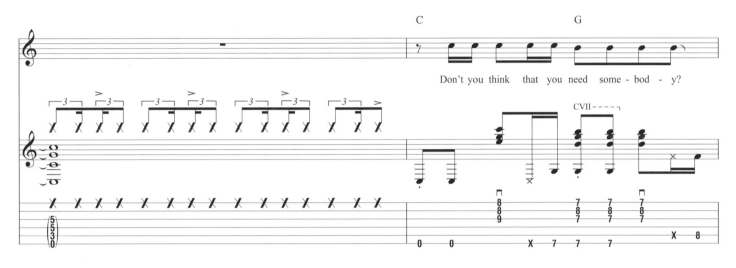

Don't you think that you need some - bod - y?

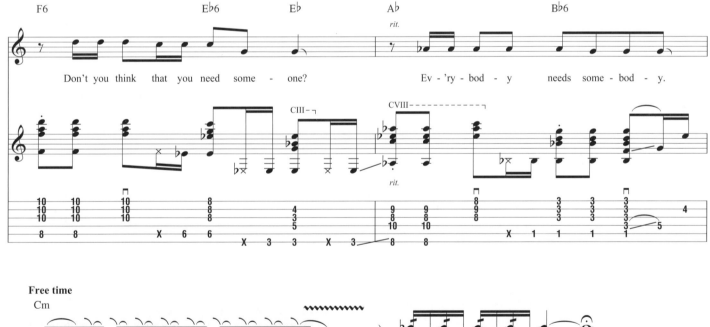

Don't you think that you need some - one? Ev - 'ry - bod - y needs some - bod - y.

Free time

Cm

*2nd string sounded by pull-off.

**Tremolo (ami)

***2nd string played w/ thumb.

Road Trippin'

Words and Music by Anthony Kiedis, Flea, John Frusciante and Chad Smith

Tune down 1/2 step:
(low to high) E♭-A♭-D♭-G♭-B♭-E♭

*Refers to downstemmed notes only.

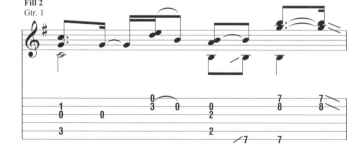

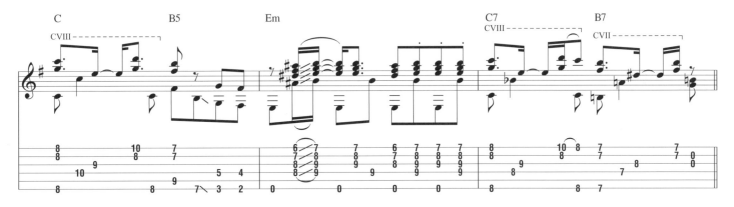

§ **C**

2nd time, Gtr. 1: w/ Fill 1

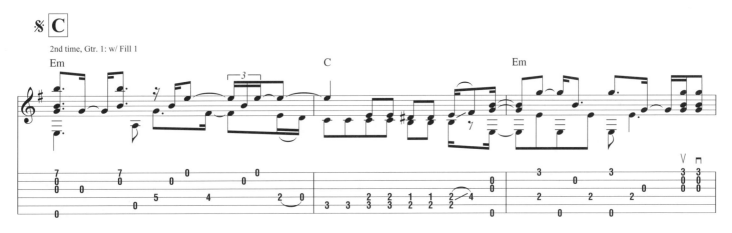

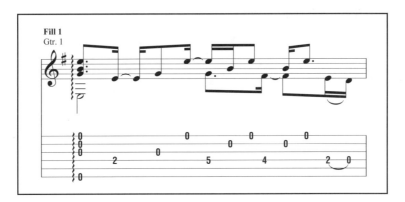

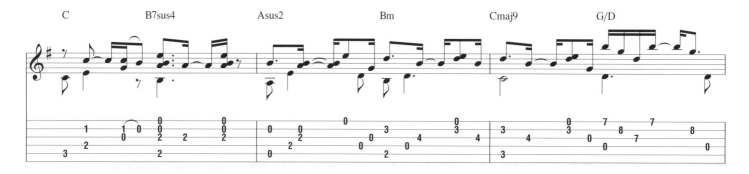

*Refers to downstemmed notes only.

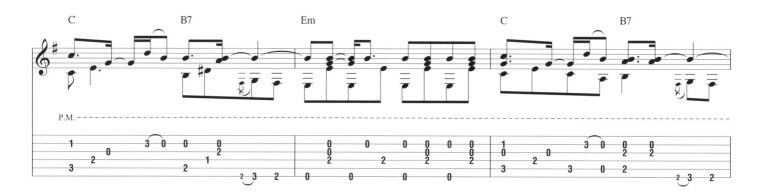

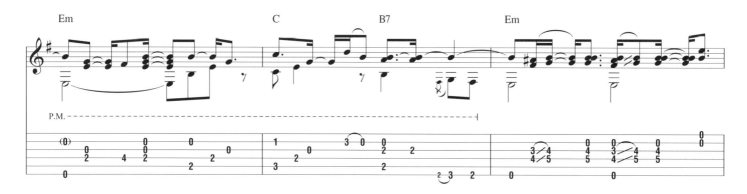

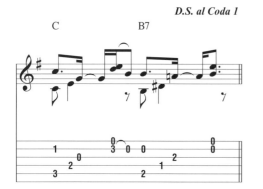

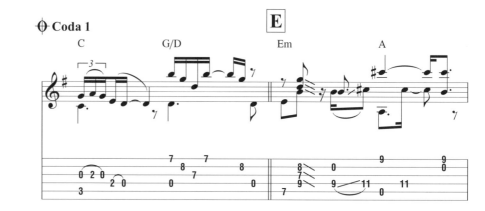

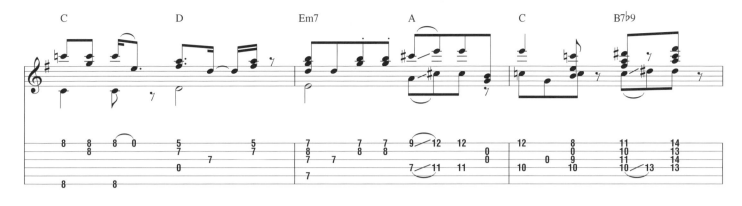

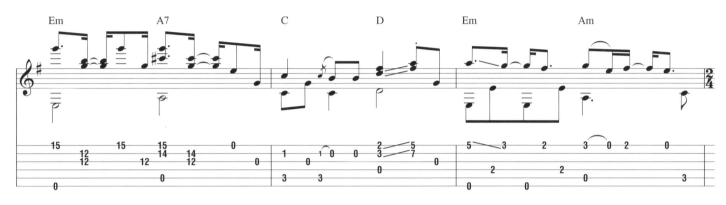

D.S.S. al Coda 2

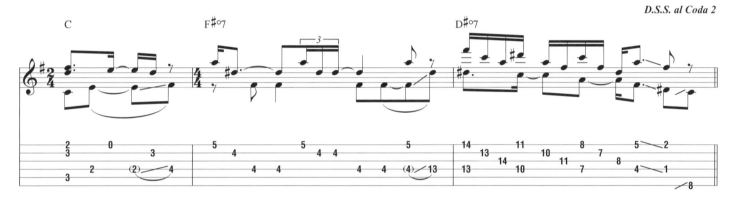

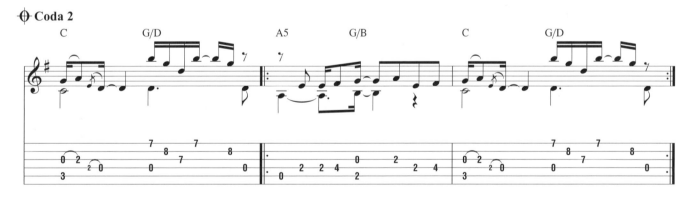

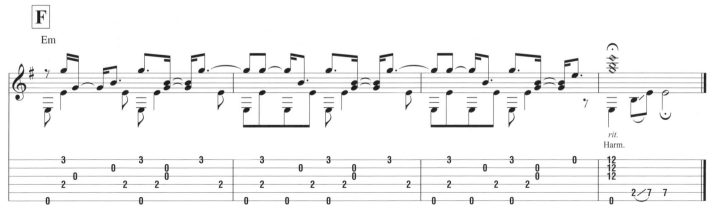

Snuff

Words and Music by Slipknot

Tune down 1 1/2 steps:
(low to high) C#-F#-B-E-G#-C#

*Rasgueado (ami), throughout.

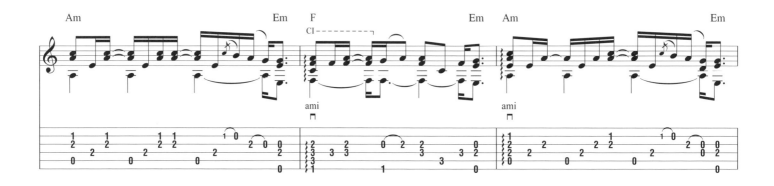

**Strike muted strings
w/ side of thumb.

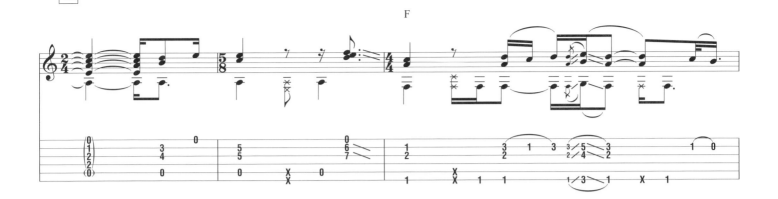

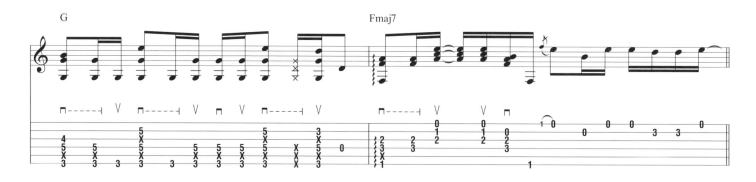

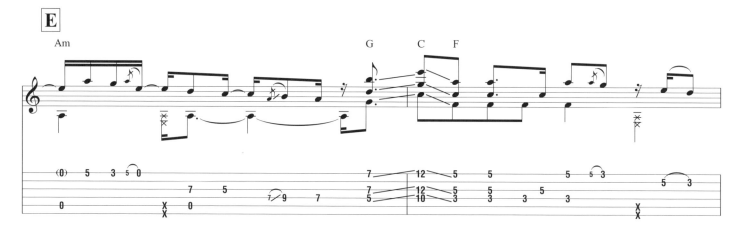

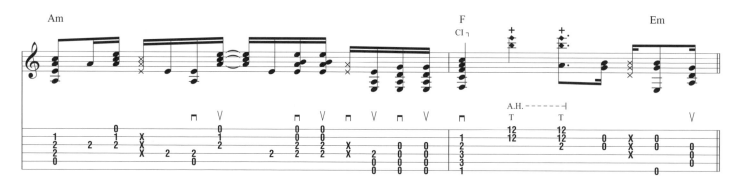

F

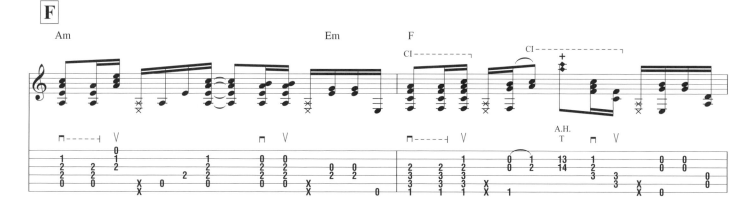

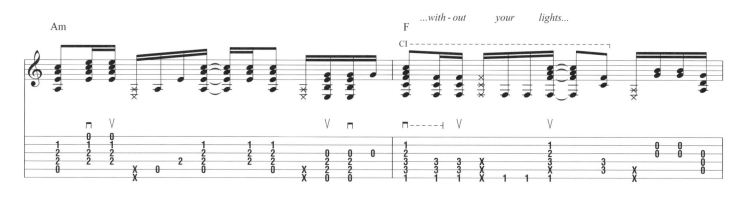

...with - out   your   lights...

...when you re - fuse to fight.

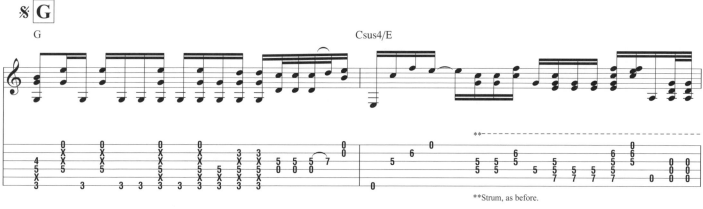

*Strum like holding a pick, next 3 meas.

§ G

**Strum, as before.

To Coda ⊕

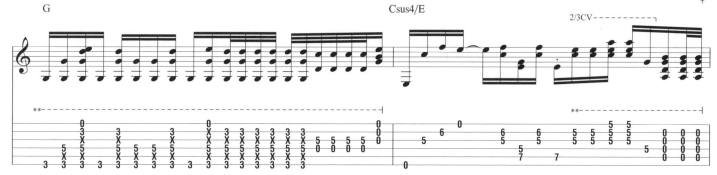

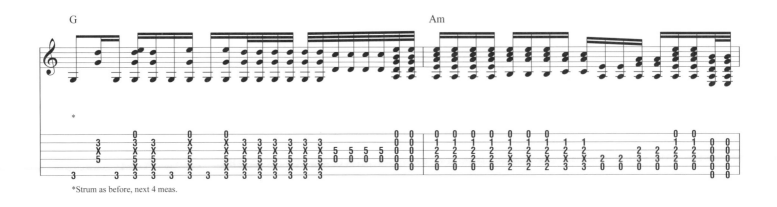

*Strum as before, next 4 meas.

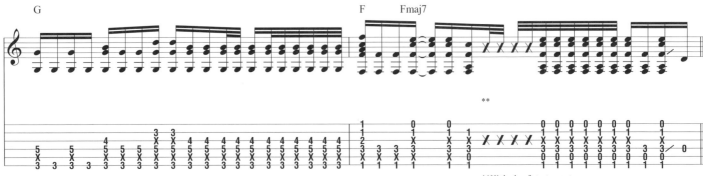

**Hit body of gtr. to create
a percussive sound.

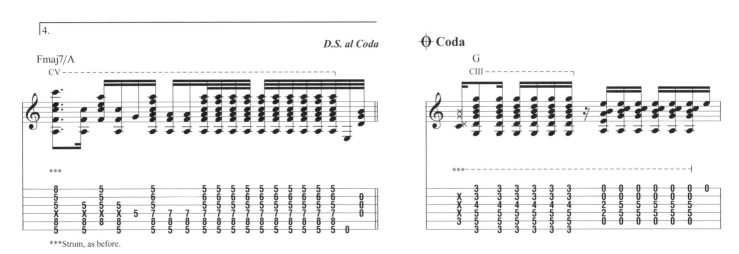

***Strum, as before.

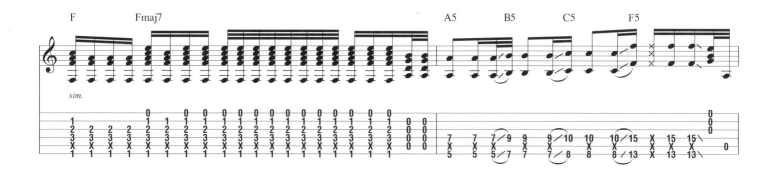

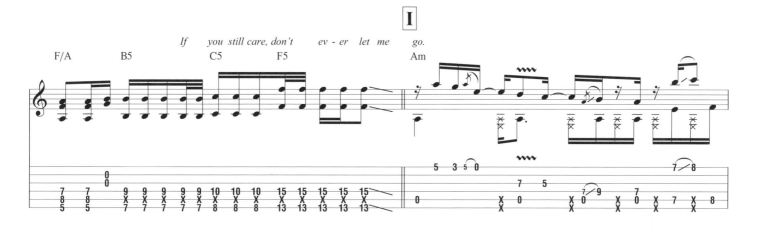

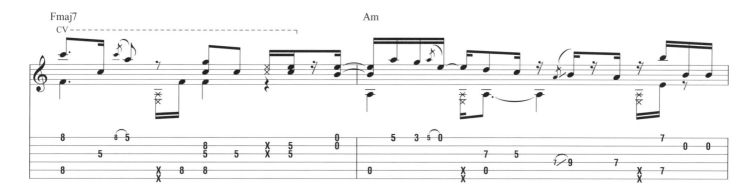

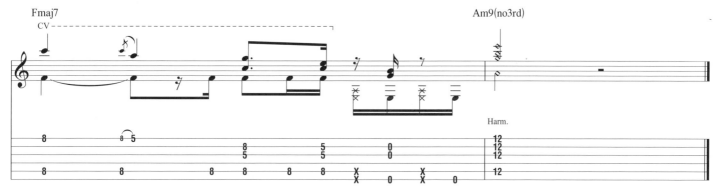

So Far Away

Words and Music by Matthew Sanders, Jonathan Seward, Brian Haner, Jr. and Zachary Baker

Tune down 1/2 step:
(low to high) Eb-Ab-Db-Gb-Bb-Eb

A

Moderately slow ♩ = 80

*Drag back of thumbnail across
strings towards ceiling.

**S=Slap strings near bridge w/ thumb.

***Single strike w/ backs of fingernails,
throughout, except where otherwise indicated.

†Hit body of gtr.

††Hit string w/ pick-hand thumb, throughout.

†††Rasgueado (ami)

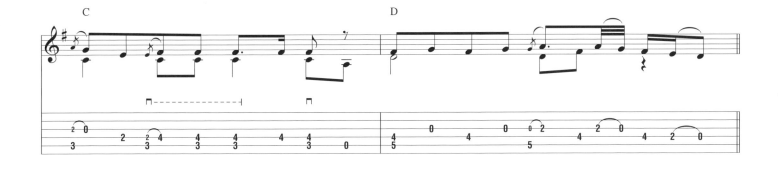

B

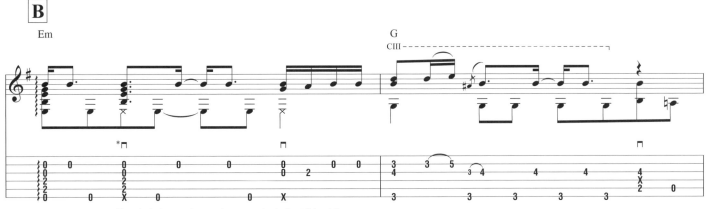

*In a single downstroke, sound upstemmed notes by striking strings
w/ backs of fingernails while slapping thumb against strings to produce
a percussive sound (downstemmed notes), throughout.

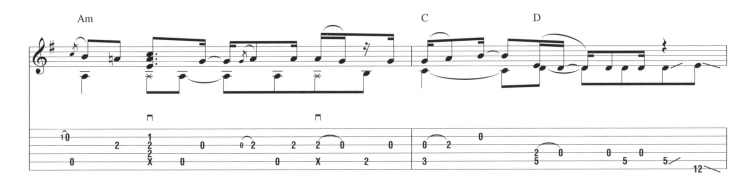

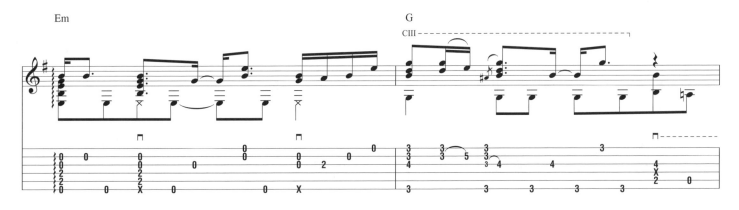

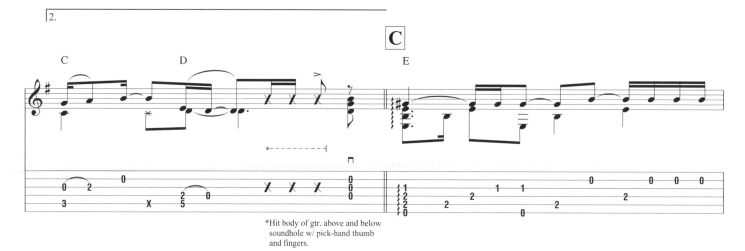

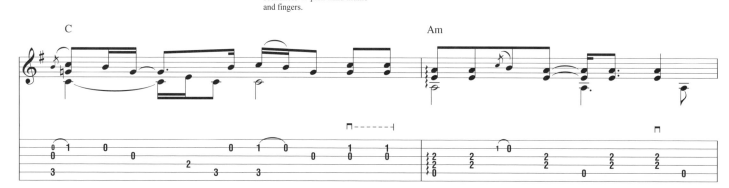

*Hit body of gtr. above and below
soundhole w/ pick-hand thumb
and fingers.

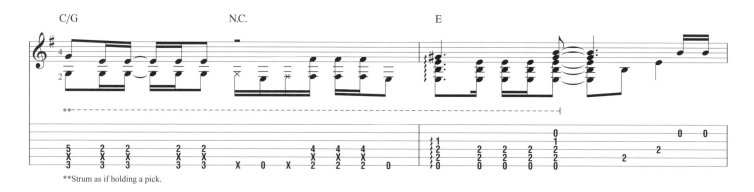

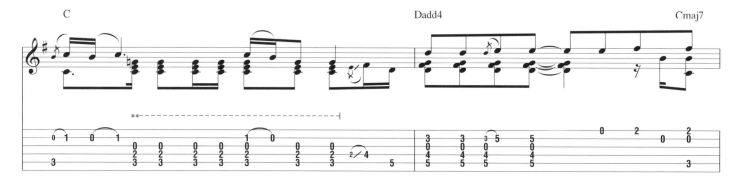

**Strum as if holding a pick.

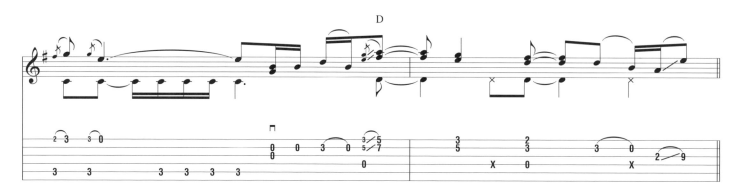

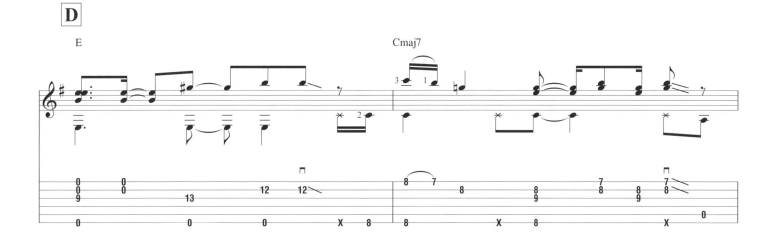

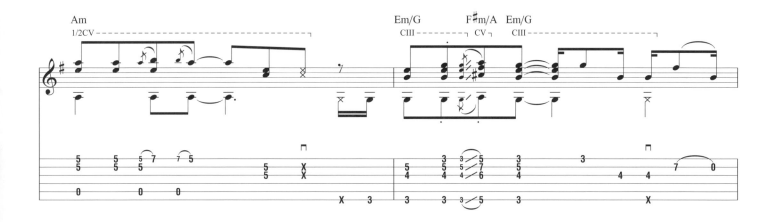

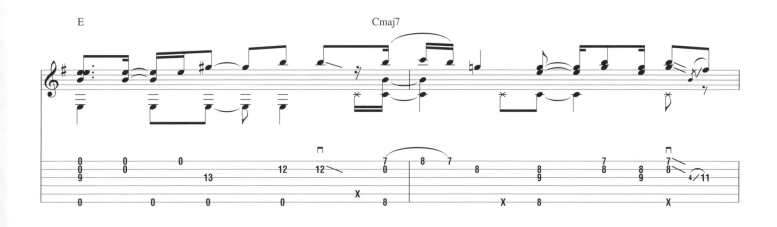

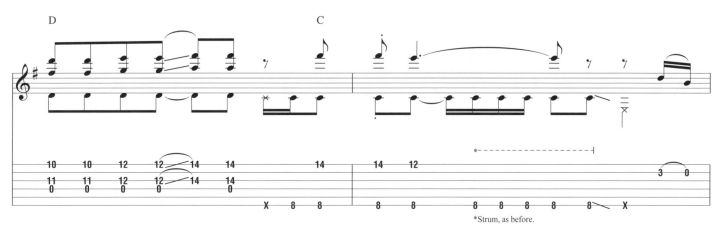

*Strum, as before.

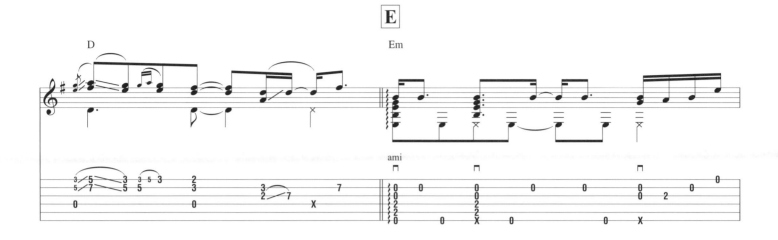

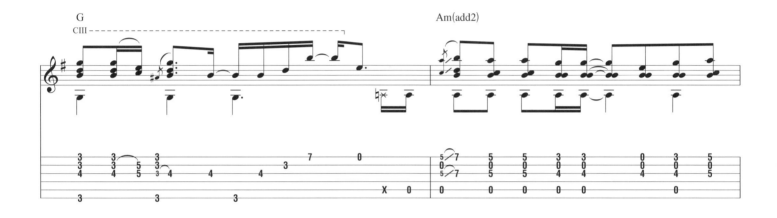

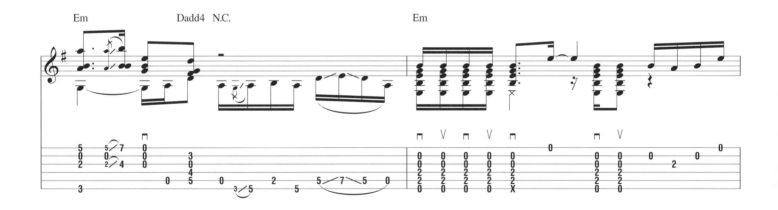

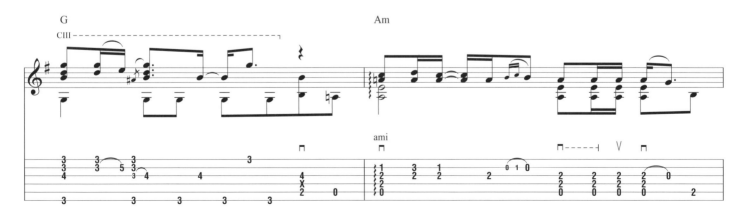

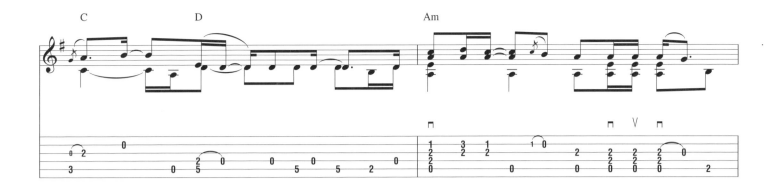

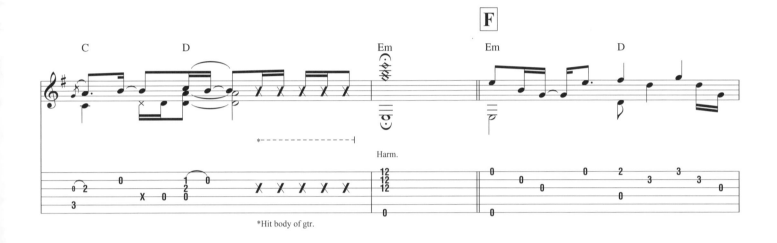

*Hit body of gtr.

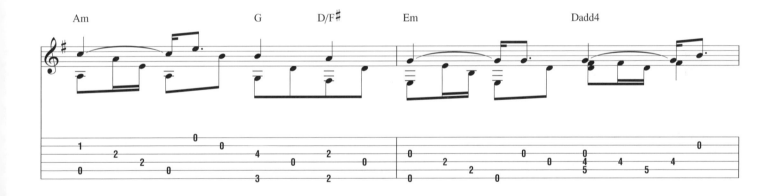

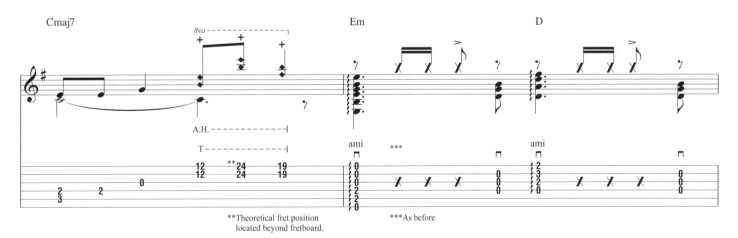

**Theoretical fret position
located beyond fretboard.

***As before

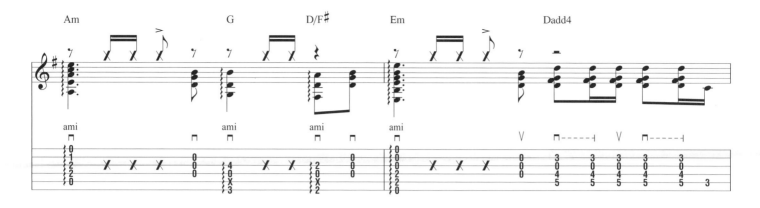

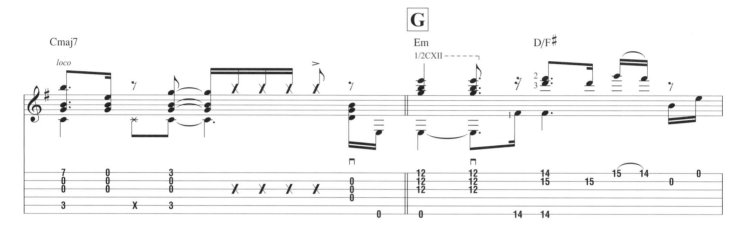

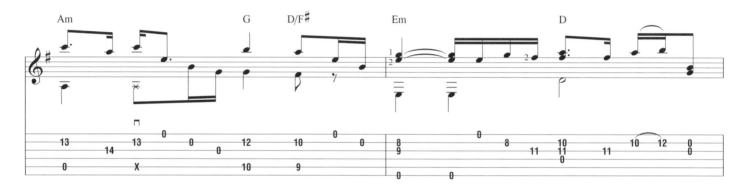

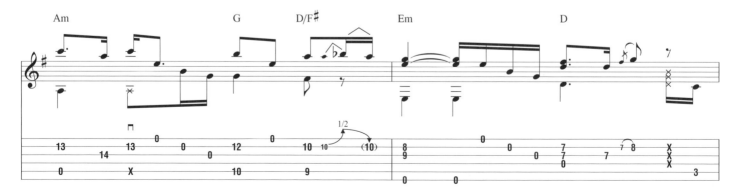

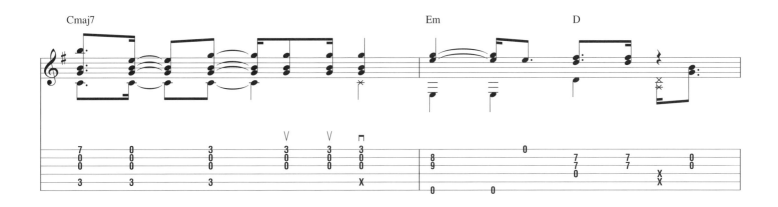

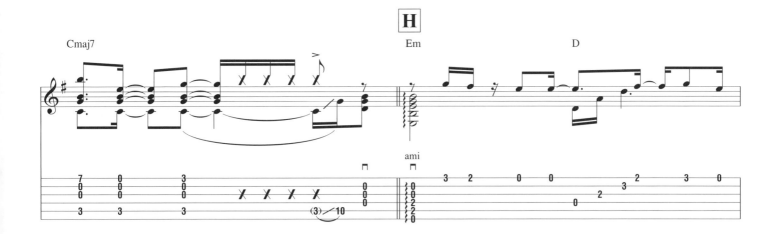

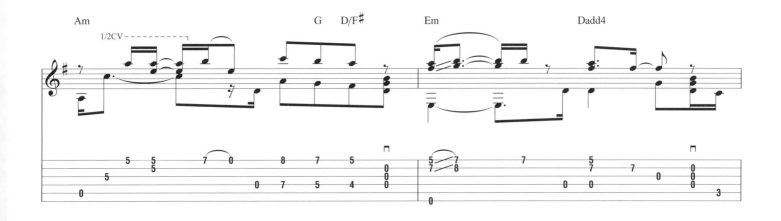

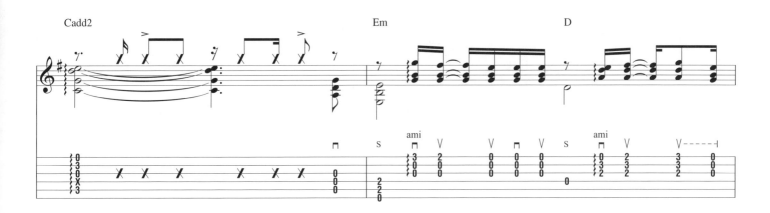

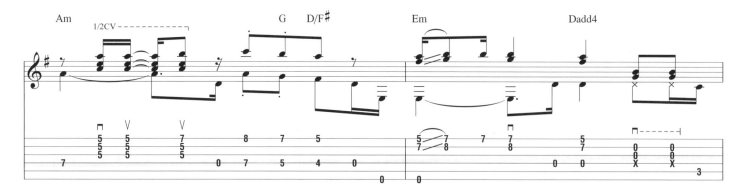

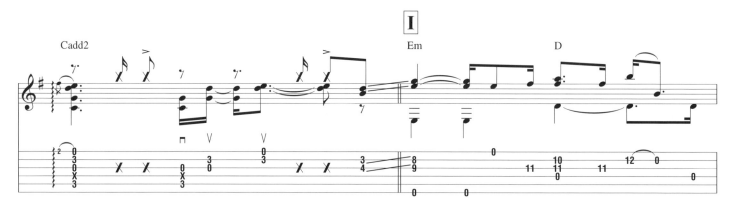

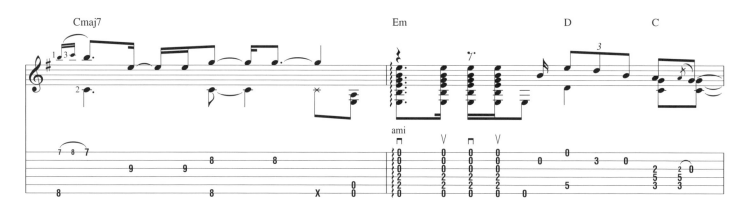

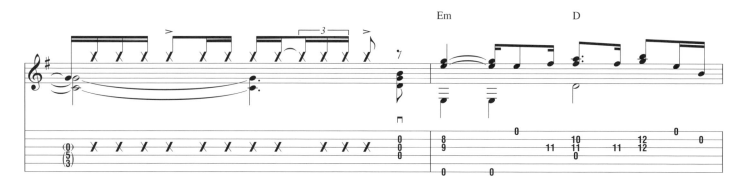

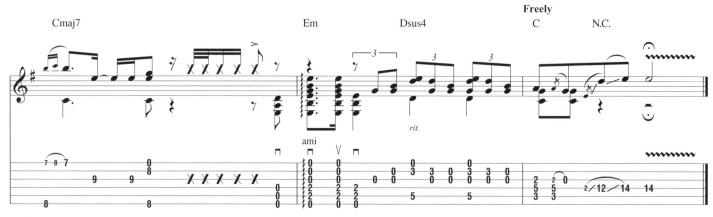

Sultans of Swing

Words and Music by Mark Knopfler

*Drop D tuning, down 1/2 step, Cutaway Capo V:
(low to high) Db-Ab-Db-Gb-Bb-Eb

Intro
Fast ♩ = 150

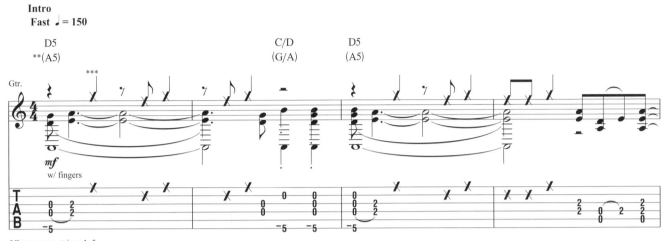

*Capo covers strings 1–5.

**Symbols in parentheses represent chord names respective to capoed guitar.
Symbols above reflect actual sounding chord. Capoed fret is "0" in tab.
Negative numbers on the 6th str. represent fretted notes played below the cutaway capo.

***Hit body of gtr. w/ right hand to create percussive sound.

†Strike strings w/ back of fingernails.

Verse

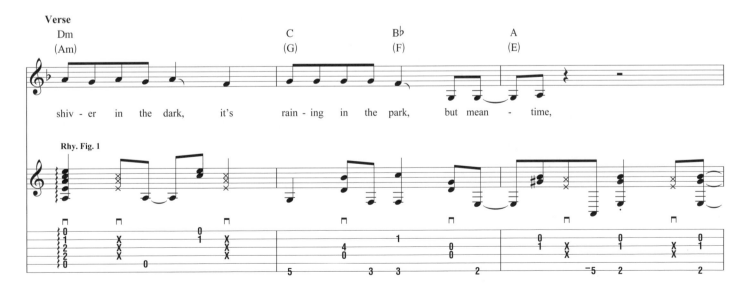

shiv - er in the dark, it's rain - ing in the park, but mean - time,

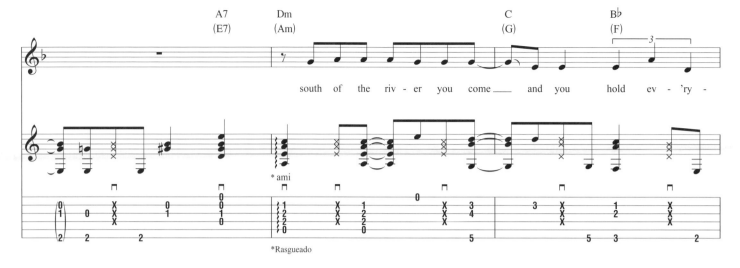

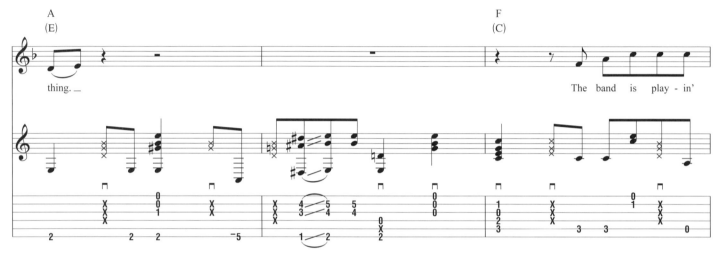

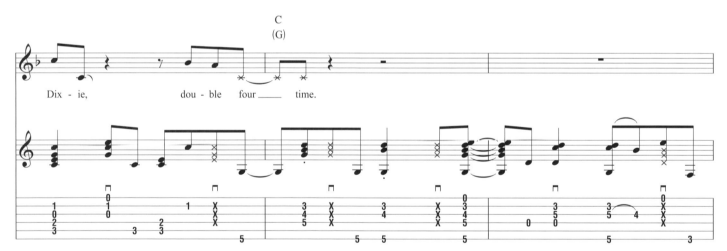

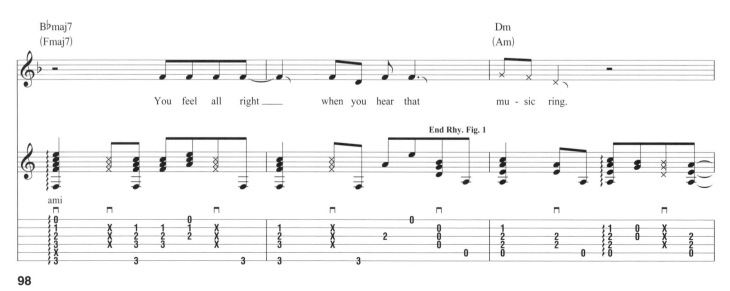

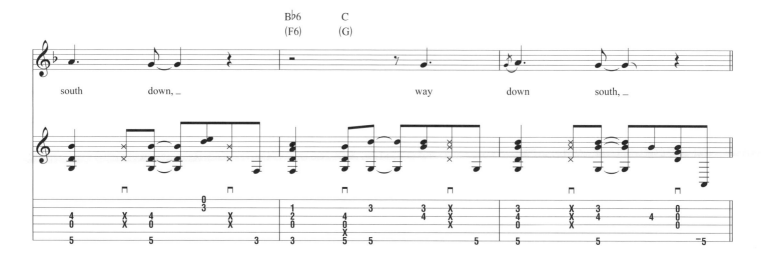

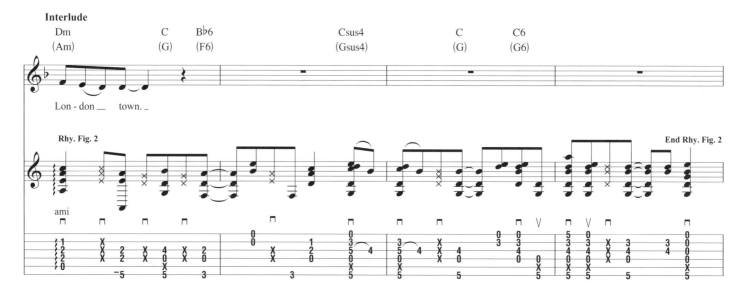

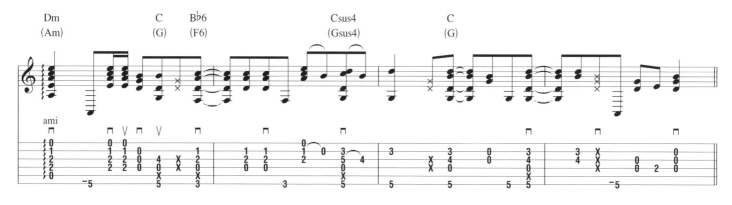

It's just the rhy - thm __ he does-n't wan-na make her __ cry or sing.__

Gtr. 1: w/ Rhy. Fig. 1 (last 6 meas.)

And his old ____ gui - tar ____ that he ____ can af - ford __

__ when he gets un - der the lights to play his thing. __

Gtr. 1

Verse

Gtr. 1: w/ Rhy. Fig. 1 (1st 6 meas.)

4. And Har - ry does-n't mind if he does-n't make __ the scene. __

__ He's got a day - time job, he's do - in' al - right. __

Interlude

Gtr. 1: w/ Rhy. Fig. 2 (1 3/4 times)

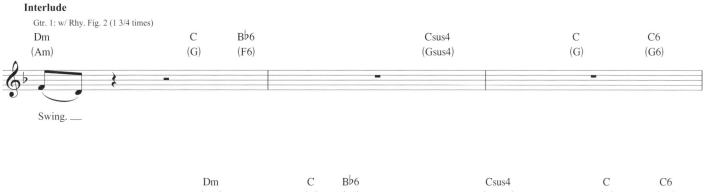

Guitar Solo

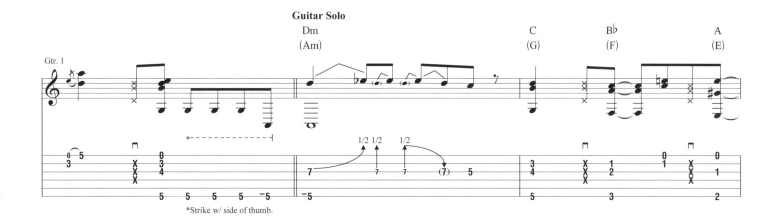

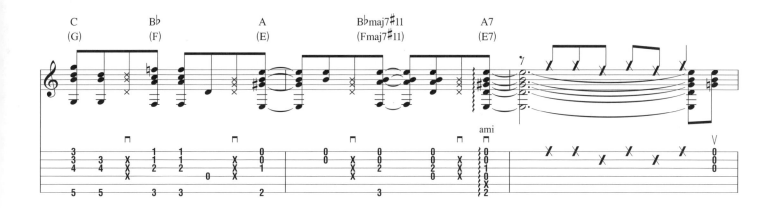

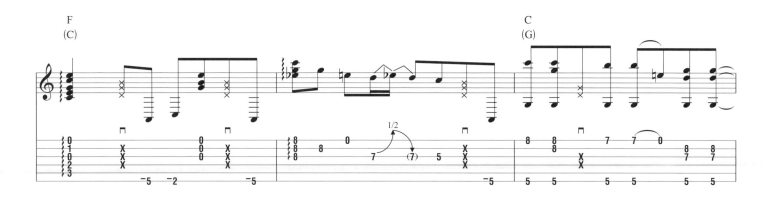

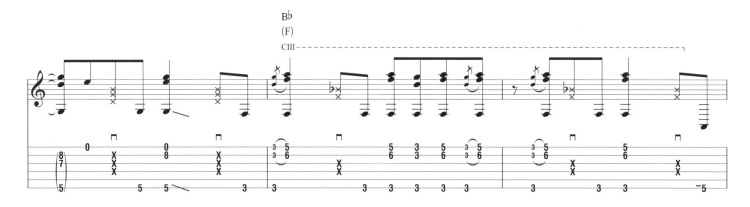

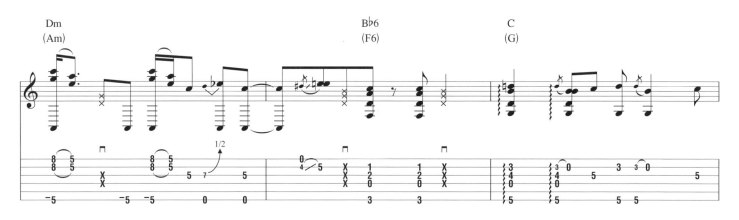

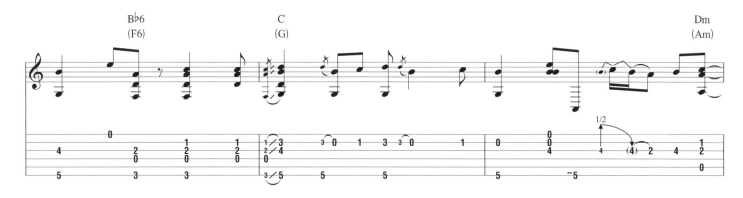

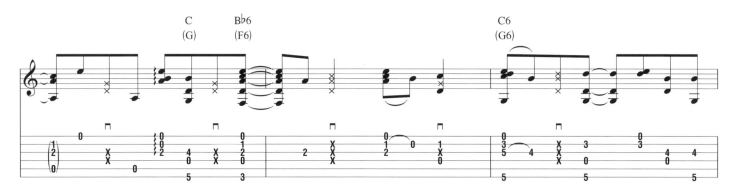

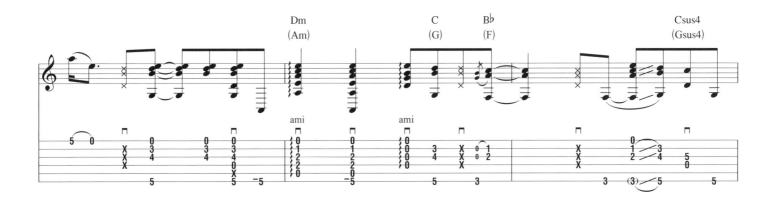

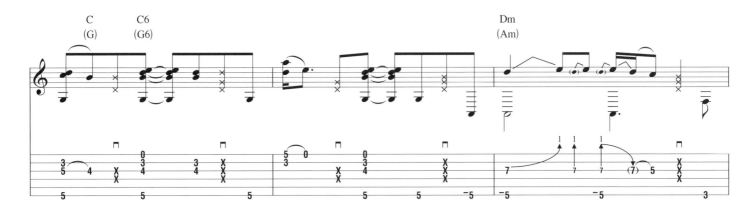

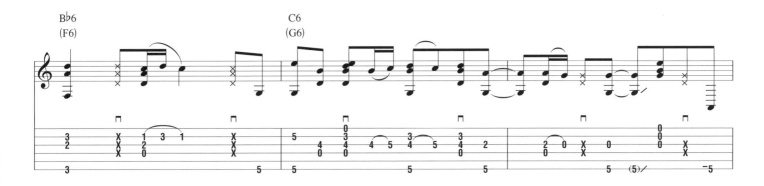

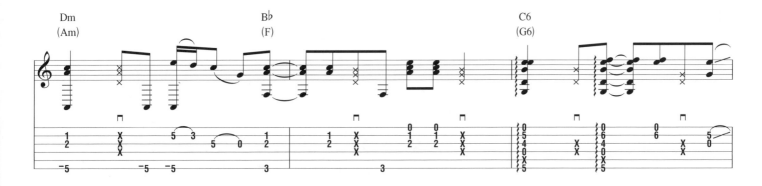

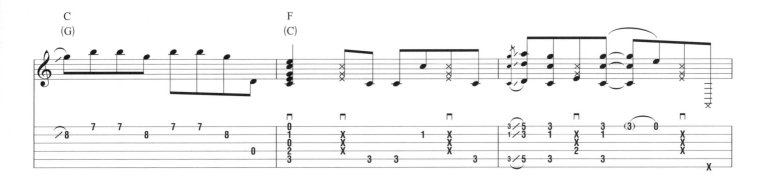

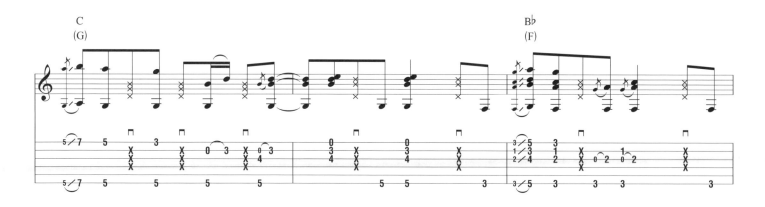

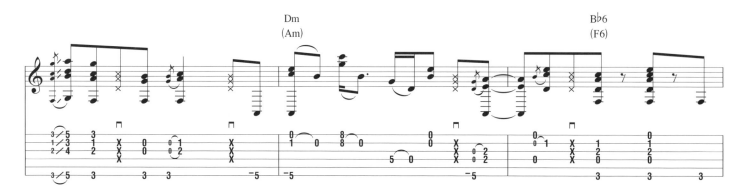

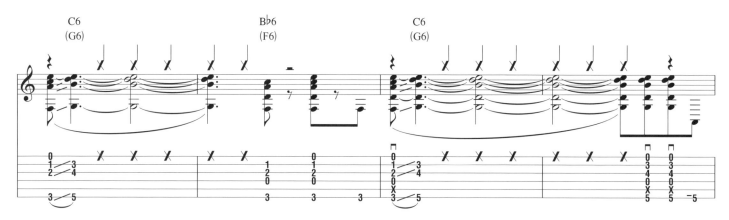

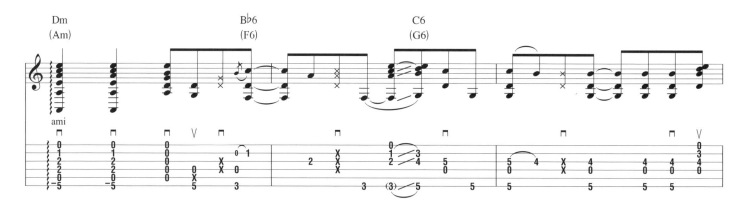

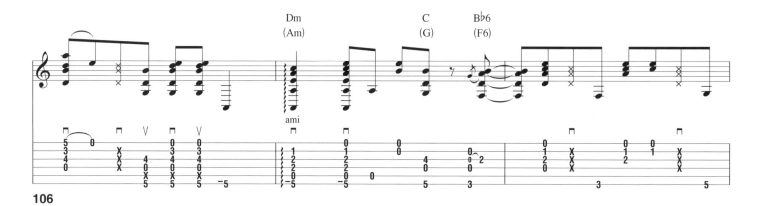

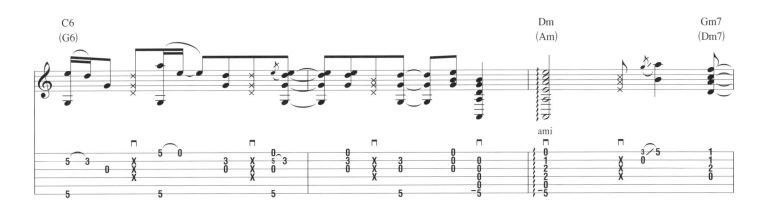

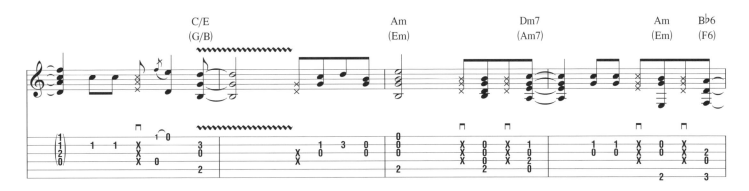

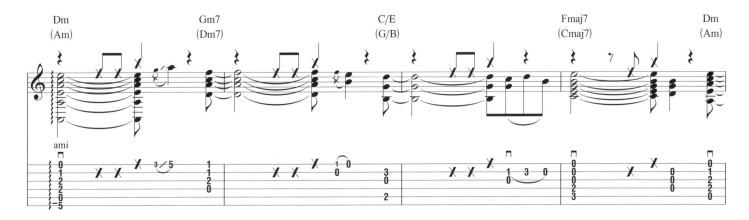

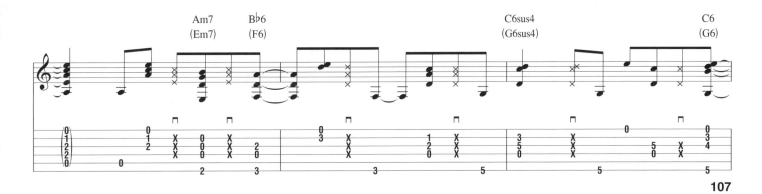

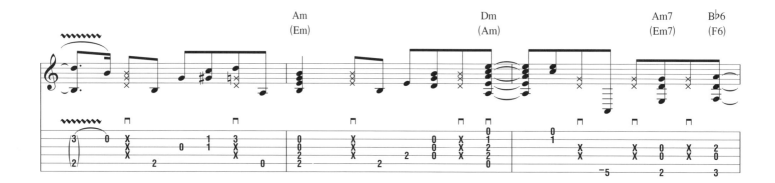

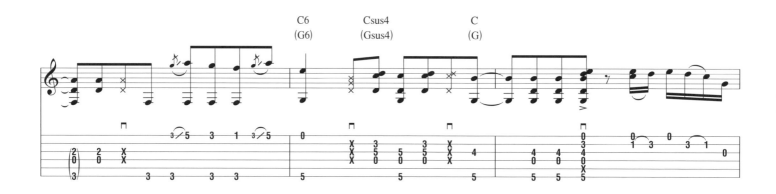

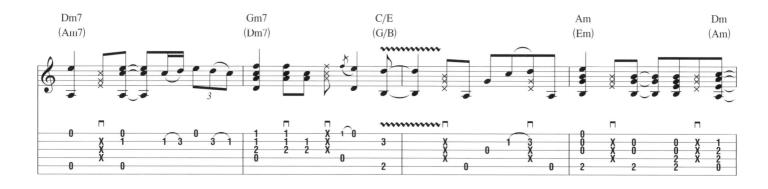

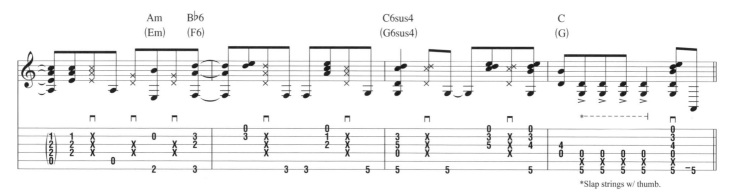

*Slap strings w/ thumb.

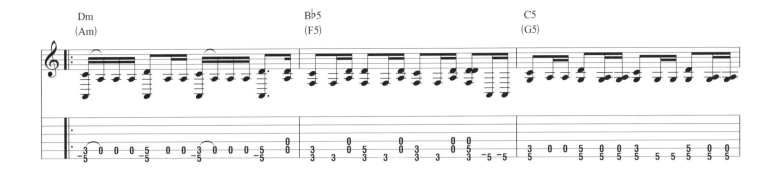

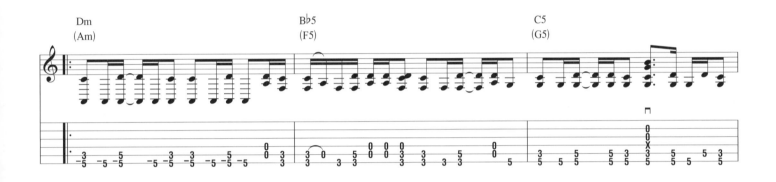

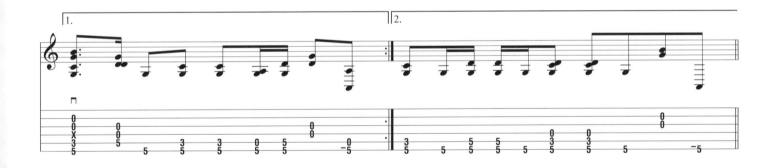

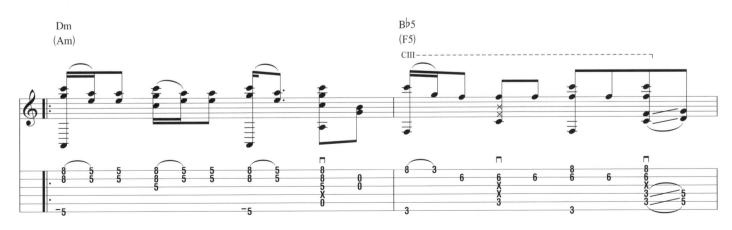

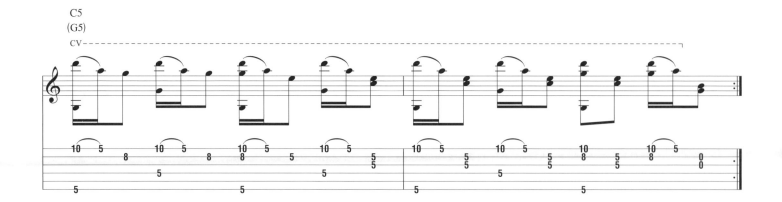

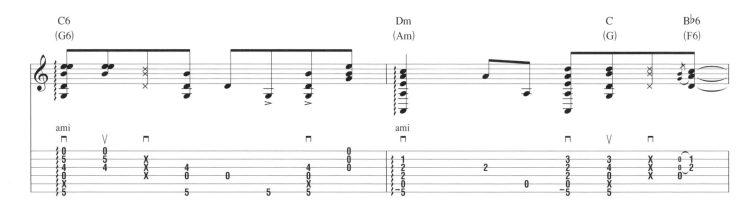

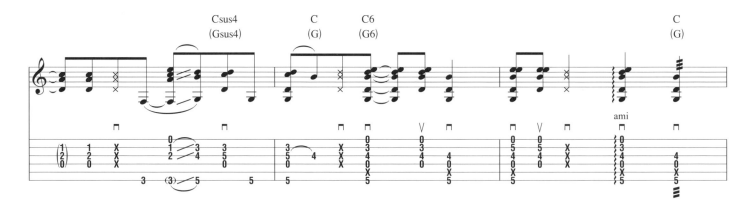

Free time

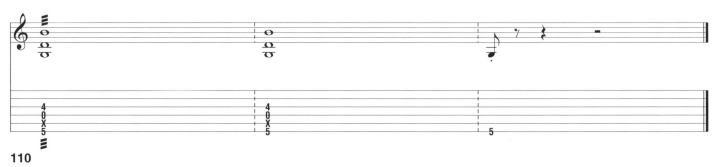

Thunderstruck

Words and Music by Angus Young and Malcolm Young

Tune down 1/2 step:
(low to high) Eb-Ab-Db-Gb-Bb-Eb

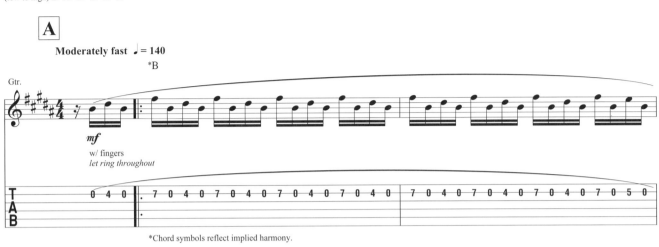

*Chord symbols reflect implied harmony.

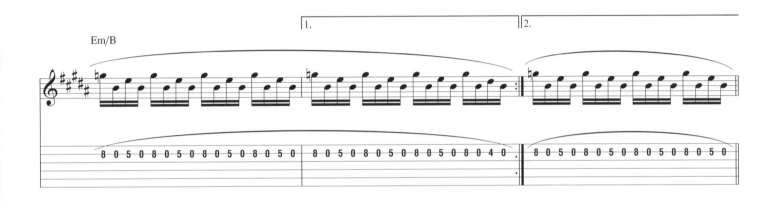

Oh, whoa.

**Hit body of gtr. w/ fingers.

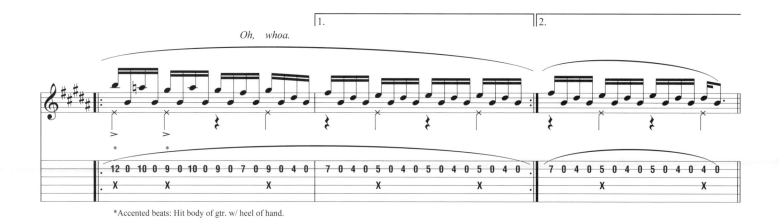

*Accented beats: Hit body of gtr. w/ heel of hand.

B

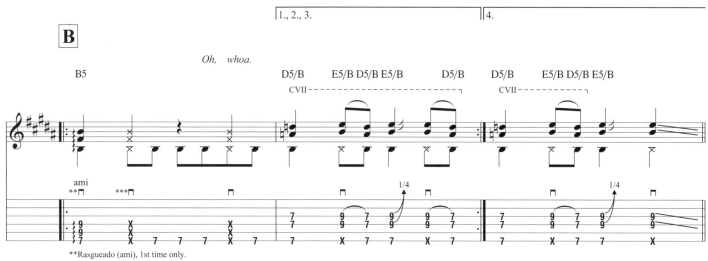

**Rasgueado (ami), 1st time only.

***In a single downstroke, sound upstemmed notes by striking strings
w/ backs of fingernails while slapping thumb against strings to
produce a percussive sound (downstemmed notes), throughout.

C

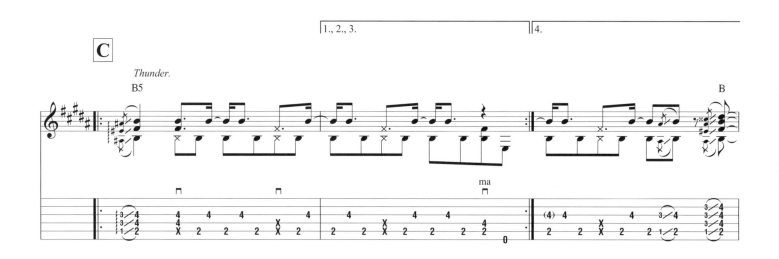

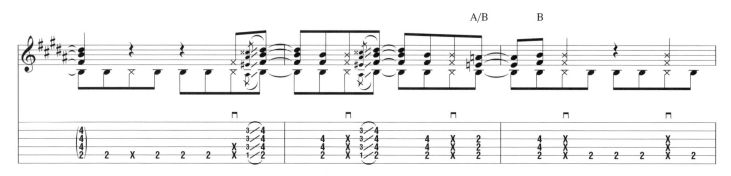

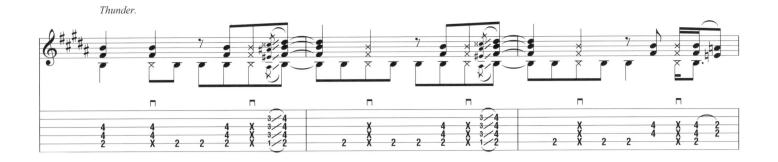

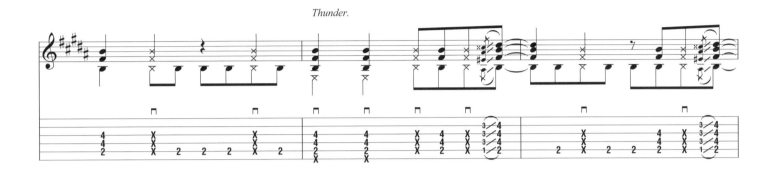

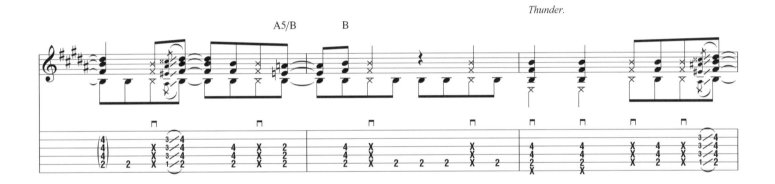

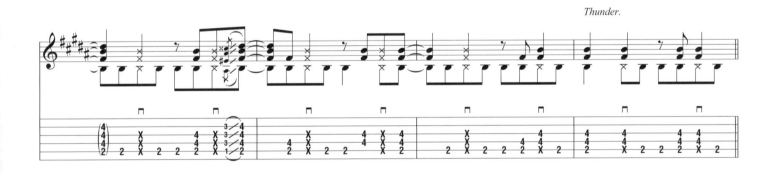

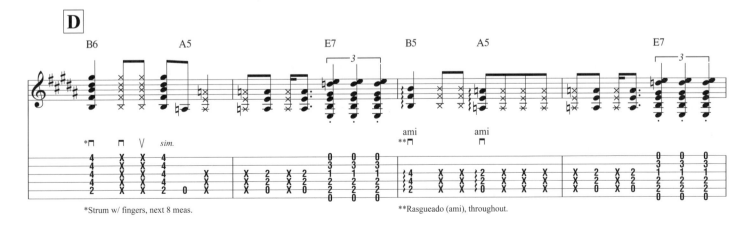

*Strum w/ fingers, next 8 meas.   **Rasgueado (ami), throughout.

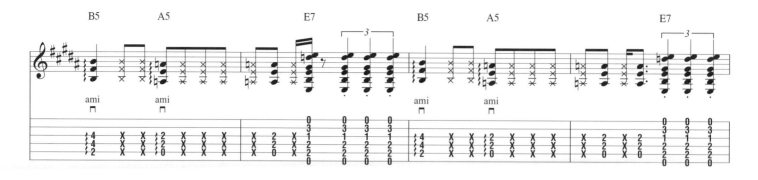

E

Thunderstruck.

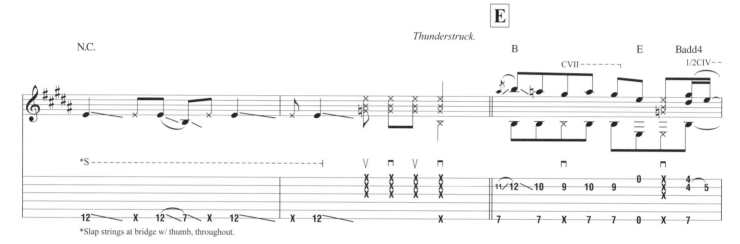

*Slap strings at bridge w/ thumb, throughout.

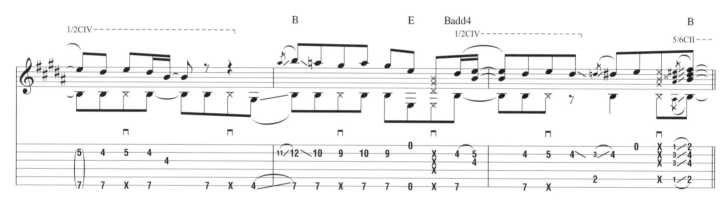

F

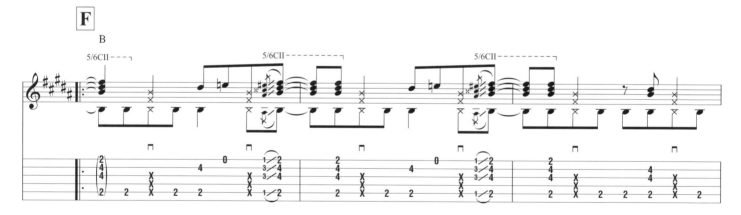

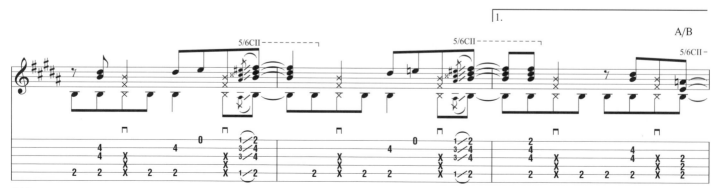

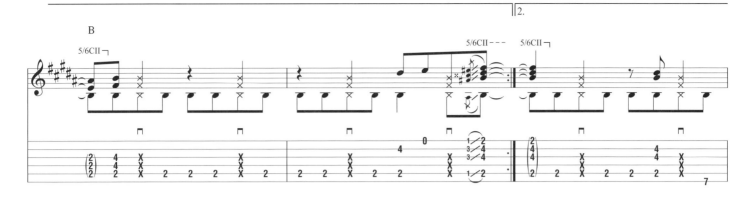

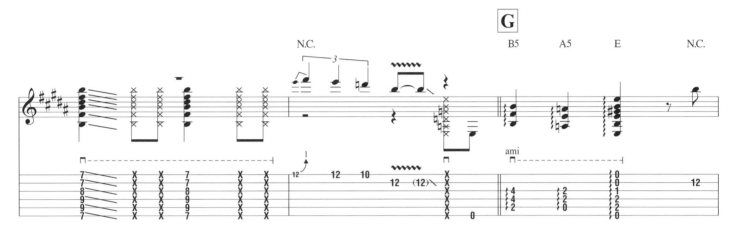

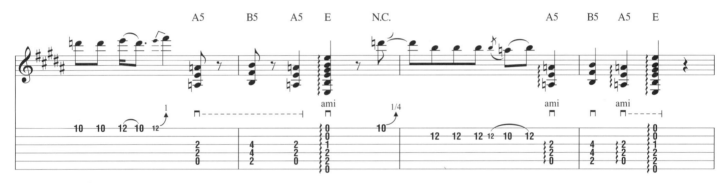

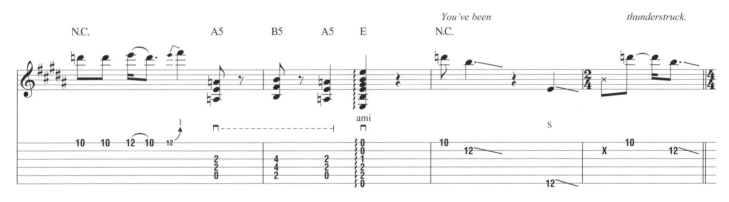

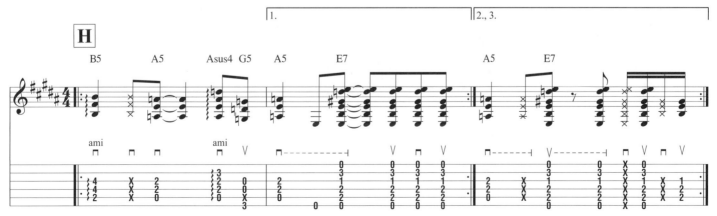

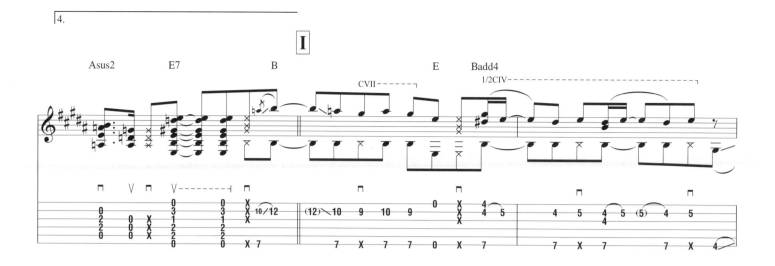

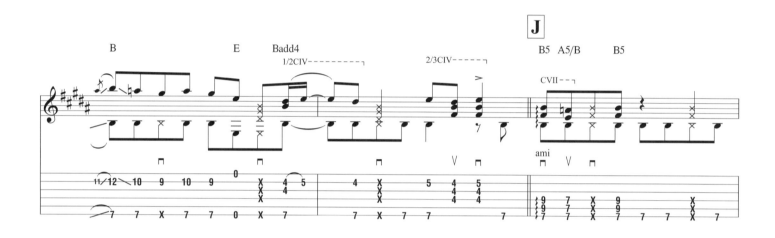

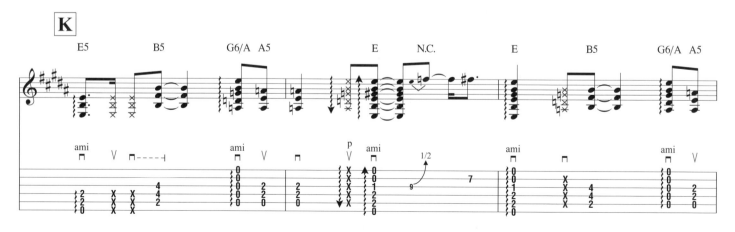

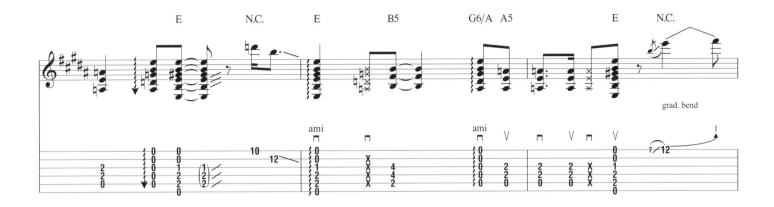

L

Oh, whoa.

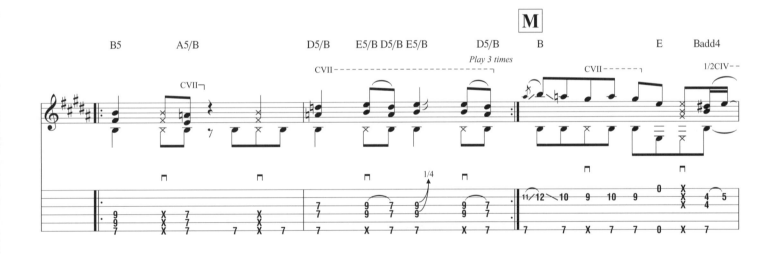

M

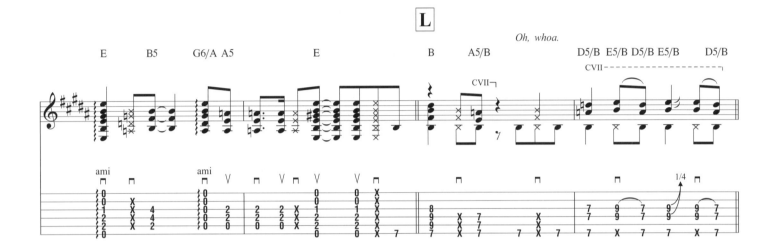

N

Thunderstruck.

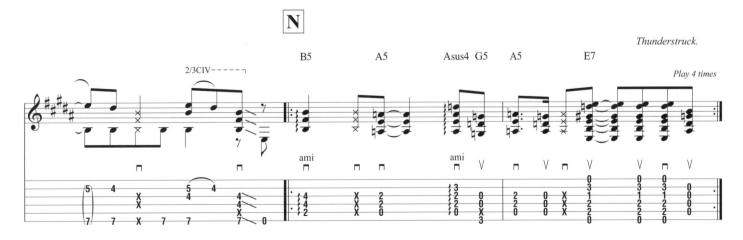

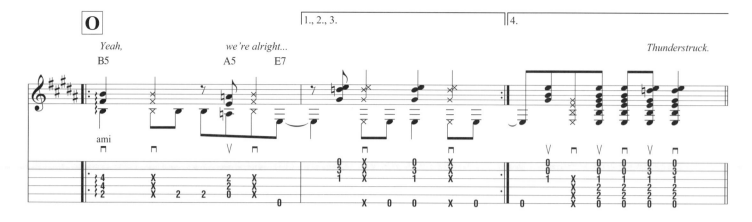

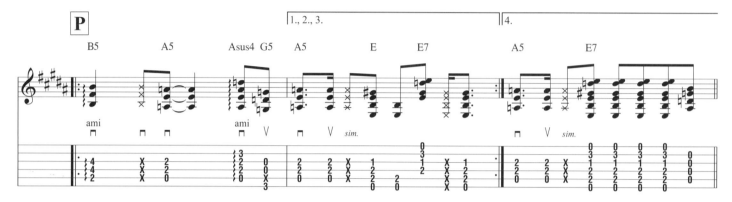

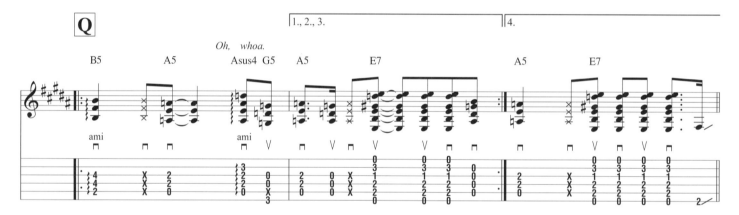

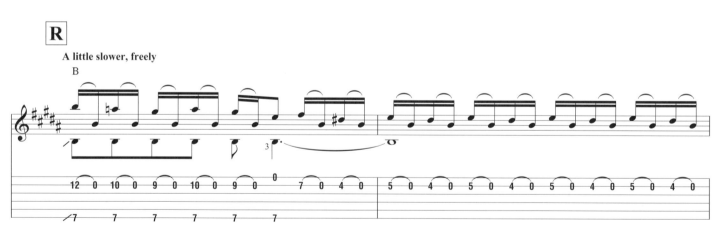

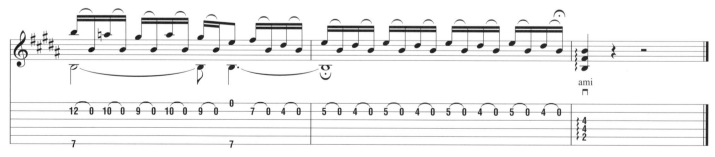

GUITAR NOTATION LEGEND

Guitar music can be notated three different ways: on a *musical staff*, in *tablature*, and in *rhythm slashes*.

RHYTHM SLASHES are written above the staff. Strum chords in the rhythm indicated. Use the chord diagrams found at the top of the first page of the transcription for the appropriate chord voicings. Round noteheads indicate single notes.

THE MUSICAL STAFF shows pitches and rhythms and is divided by bar lines into measures. Pitches are named after the first seven letters of the alphabet.

TABLATURE graphically represents the guitar fingerboard. Each horizontal line represents a string, and each number represents a fret.

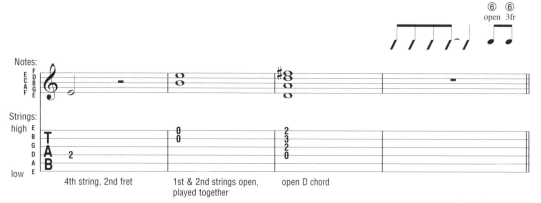

4th string, 2nd fret | 1st & 2nd strings open, played together | open D chord

HALF-STEP BEND: Strike the note and bend up 1/2 step.

WHOLE-STEP BEND: Strike the note and bend up one step.

GRACE NOTE BEND: Strike the note and immediately bend up as indicated.

SLIGHT (MICROTONE) BEND: Strike the note and bend up 1/4 step.

BEND AND RELEASE: Strike the note and bend up as indicated, then release back to the original note. Only the first note is struck.

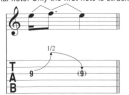

PRE-BEND: Bend the note as indicated, then strike it.

VIBRATO: The string is vibrated by rapidly bending and releasing the note with the fretting hand.

WIDE VIBRATO: The pitch is varied to a greater degree by vibrating with the fretting hand.

HAMMER-ON: Strike the first (lower) note with one finger, then sound the higher note (on the same string) with another finger by fretting it without picking.

PULL-OFF: Place both fingers on the notes to be sounded. Strike the first note and without picking, pull the finger off to sound the second (lower) note.

LEGATO SLIDE: Strike the first note and then slide the same fret-hand finger up or down to the second note. The second note is not struck.

SHIFT SLIDE: Same as legato slide, except the second note is struck.

TRILL: Very rapidly alternate between the notes indicated by continuously hammering on and pulling off.

TAPPING: Hammer ("tap") the fret indicated with the pick-hand index or middle finger and pull off to the note fretted by the fret hand.

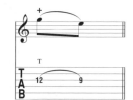

NATURAL HARMONIC: Strike the note while the fret-hand lightly touches the string directly over the fret indicated.

Harm.

PINCH HARMONIC: The note is fretted normally and a harmonic is produced by adding the edge of the thumb or the tip of the index finger of the pick hand to the normal pick attack.

P.H.

PICK SCRAPE: The edge of the pick is rubbed down (or up) the string, producing a scratchy sound.

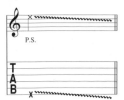

P.S.

MUFFLED STRINGS: A percussive sound is produced by laying the fret hand across the string(s) without depressing, and striking them with the pick hand.

PALM MUTING: The note is partially muted by the pick hand lightly touching the string(s) just before the bridge.

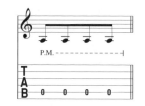

P.M. ––––––––––––

RAKE: Drag the pick across the strings indicated with a single motion.

rake – – –|

TREMOLO PICKING: The note is picked as rapidly and continuously as possible.

VIBRATO BAR DIVE AND RETURN: The pitch of the note or chord is dropped a specified number of steps (in rhythm), then returned to the original pitch.

w/ bar

VIBRATO BAR SCOOP: Depress the bar just before striking the note, then quickly release the bar.

w/ bar – – – – – – – –|

VIBRATO BAR DIP: Strike the note and then immediately drop a specified number of steps, then release back to the original pitch.

w/ bar

EXPAND YOUR ACOUSTIC GUITAR KNOWLEDGE

THE HAL LEONARD ACOUSTIC GUITAR METHOD
by Chad Johnson

This method uses real songs to teach you all the basics of acoustic guitar in the style of the Beatles, Eric Clapton, John Mellencamp, James Taylor and many others. Lessons include: strumming; fingerpicking; using a capo; open tunings; folk, country & bluegrass styles; acoustic blues; acoustic rock; and more.
00697347 Book/Online Audio $16.99

DVD ACOUSTIC GUITAR

Acoustic Guitar – At a Glance features four lessons, including: Strumming Chords, Fingerstyle Basics, Travis Picking, and Capo Basics and uses the riffs of 16 songs, including: Brown Eyed Girl • Dust in the Wind • Free Fallin' • Landslide • Maggie May • Norwegian Wood (This Bird Has Flown) • Yesterday • and more.
00696017 Book/DVD Pack $9.99

ACOUSTIC GUITAR CHORDS
by Chad Johnson

Acoustic Guitar Chords teaches you the must-know chords that will get you strumming quickly. The included DVD demonstrates each chord and all the examples are accompanied by a full band, so you can hear these chords in the proper context. Teaches: open chords, barre chords, seventh chords, other chord types (suspended, add9), open-string drone chords, full song examples, and more.
00696484 Book/DVD Pack $9.99

HAL LEONARD BLUEGRASS GUITAR METHOD
by Fred Sokolow

This book uses popular bluegrass songs to teach you the basics of rhythm and lead playing in the styles of Doc Watson, Tony Rice, Maybelle Carter, Lester Flatt, and many others. Lessons include Carter strumming, alternating bass, waltz strums, using the capo, hammer-ons, pull-offs, slides, crosspicking, and more. Songs include: Amazing Grace • Blue Moon of Kentucky • Cripple Creek • I Am a Man of Constant Sorrow • I'll Fly Away • We'll Meet Again Sweetheart • The Wreck of the Old '97 • and more.
00697405 Book/Online Audio $16.99

HAL LEONARD FINGERSTYLE GUITAR METHOD
by Chad Johnson

The *Hal Leonard Fingerstyle Guitar Method* is your complete guide to learning fingerstyle guitar. Songs covered include: Annie's Song • Blowin' in the Wind • Dust in the Wind • Fire and Rain • Georgia on My Mind • Imagine • Landslide • Tears in Heaven • What a Wonderful World • Yesterday • You've Got a Friend • and more.
00697378 Book/Online Audio $19.99

HAL LEONARD FOLK GUITAR METHOD
by Fred Sokolow

You'll learn: basic strumming; strumming variations; Carter-style flatpicking; bass runs; basic fingerstyle patterns; alternating thumb patterns; flatpicking solos; hammer-ons and pull-offs; fingerpicking solos; using a capo; I-IV-V chord families; and much more. Songs include: Blowin' in the Wind • Freight Train • The House of the Rising Sun • Leaving on a Jet Plane • This Land Is Your Land • and more.
00697414 Book/Online Audio $14.99

FRETBOARD ROADMAPS – BLUEGRASS AND FOLK GUITAR
by Fred Sokolow

This book/CD pack will have you playing lead and rhythm anywhere on the fretboard, in any key. You'll learn chord-based licks, moveable major and blues scales, major pentatonic "sliding scales," first-position major scales, and moveable-position major scales. The book includes easy-to-follow diagrams and instructions for beginning, intermediate and advanced players. The CD includes 41 demonstration tracks to help you perfect your new skills.
00695355 Book/CD Pack................................$14.99

HAL•LEONARD®

www.halleonard.com

Prices, contents, and availability subject to change without notice.

FRETBOARD ROADMAPS FOR ACOUSTIC GUITAR
by Fred Sokolow

Learn to play lead, rhythm, chords & progressions anywhere on the fretboard, in any key and in a variety of styles. Each chapter presents a pattern and shows how to use it, along with playing tips and guitar insights. For beginning to advanced players, with a CD featuring demos of all the exercises, plus practice tracks to help you learn six different soloing techniques.
00695940 Book/CD Pack................................$16.99

100 ACOUSTIC LESSONS
by Chad Johnson and Michael Mueller

Featuring 100 individual modules covering a giant array of topics, each lesson in this Acoustic volume includes detailed instruction with playing examples presented in standard notation and tablature. You'll also get extremely useful tips, scale diagrams, chord grids, photos, and more to reinforce your learning experience, plus online audio featuring performance demos of all the examples in the book!
00696456 Book/Online Audio $24.99

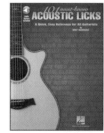

101 MUST-KNOW ACOUSTIC LICKS
by Wolf Marshall

Here are 101 definitive phrases, plus audio demonstration tracks, from every major acoustic guitar style, neatly organized into easy-to-use categories. They're all here: classical, neoclassical, Spanish, blues, pop, rock, folk, jazz, bossa nova, swing, country, ragtime, and more!
00696045 Book/Online Audio $17.99

PERCUSSIVE ACOUSTIC GUITAR METHOD
by Chris Woods

Providing detailed, step-by-step instruction on a variety of percussive guitar techniques, this book includes warm-ups, exercises, full peices, and pracitcal "how-to" training that will get you slapping, tapping, and enjoying your guitar like never before. Covers: string slapping, body percussion, tapping, harmonics, alternate tunings, standard notation and tab, and more!
00696643 Book/Online Media $19.99

TOTAL ACOUSTIC GUITAR
by Andrew DuBrock

Packed with tons of examples and audio demonstrations, this book/online audio package breaks down the most common, essential acoustic techniques with clear, concise instruction and then applies them to real-world musical riffs, licks, and songs. You'll learn syncopation, power chords, arpeggios, rhythm fills, and much more.
00696072 Book/Online Audio $19.99